Praise for
Nothing Changes *Until* **You Do**

"In *Nothing Changes Until You Do,* Mike Robbins shares ageless wisdom that is far too often overlooked because of its seeming simplicity. Don't be fooled! This book cover should be stamped in gold lettering: 'Contents 100% authentic.' Breathe deeply as these compassionate teachings open your heart."
—Michael Bernard Beckwith, author of *Life Visioning*

"*Nothing Changes Until You Do* is a powerful book that will open your mind and touch your heart. Mike Robbins's inspiring and down-to-earth wisdom can guide you to be more compassionate, kind, and loving toward yourself and everyone else in your life."
—Marci Shimoff, *New York Times* best-selling author of *Happy for No Reason*

"This book is filled with quick, compelling, and actionable ideas. Mike Robbins uses his personal experience to help all of us see how we can take small steps toward a better life. Reading this book will give you a new way to think about how you interact with the world."
—Tom Rath, *New York Times* best-selling author of *Eat Move Sleep* and *StrengthsFinder 2.0*

"*Nothing Changes Until You Do* focuses on an important and often overlooked aspect of compassion . . . having compassion for oneself. Mike Robbins's approach is both heartfelt and practical, which is why he continues to be such a popular speaker at Google."
—Chade-Meng Tan, *New York Times* best-selling author of *Search Inside Yourself,* and Google's Jolly Good Fellow

"Mike Robbins has a unique ability to open people's minds, touch their hearts, and teach valuable lessons about life and business. I have personally benefited from his work, as have so many of the people on my team."
—Jack Calhoun, president of Banana Republic

"I've had the great pleasure to witness Mike grow as a family man and as an author. As a mentor, years ago my late husband, Richard Carlson, passed a torch to Mike whom he loved like a younger brother. Mike offers such wisdom and heart in *Nothing Changes Until You Do.* These pages will thoughtfully show you how to live like he does—authentically happy and grateful for every day."
—**Kristine Carlson,** co-author to the #1 *New York Times* best-selling *Don't Sweat the Small Stuff* book series

"Mike Robbins rocks . . . he's definitely one of my 'spiritual running buddies.' *Nothing Changes Until You Do* is a beautiful book filled with wisdom that is both deep and accessible at the same time. By reading this book you'll experience more kindness, love, and acceptance for yourself and others."
—**Gabrielle Bernstein,** *New York Times* best-selling author of *May Cause Miracles*

"Mike Robbins's wisdom and insight are so important in both business and life. Self-compassion, as Mike reminds us in *Nothing Changes Until You Do,* is essential to everything we do."
—**Chip Conley,** founder of Joie de Vivre Hotels and *New York Times* best-selling author of *Peak*

"Mike Robbins lives his message. He is truly as kind, wise, generous, and joyful as he teaches us to be in *Nothing Changes Until You Do*— and that's why I trust him. This guy is onto something. I don't want to just read more of him; I want to be more like him."
—**Glennon Doyle Melton,** *New York Times* best-selling of *Carry On, Warrior* and creator of Momastery.com

"Mike Robbins is a master at teaching us how to become the best version of ourselves. I highly recommend you read this book and let it inspire you to be a better you so you can change the world for the better."
—**Jon Gordon,** author of *The Energy Bus*

"There is no shortage of self-help books on the market. What makes *Nothing Changes Until You Do* different is Mike Robbins's one-of-a-kind talent for combining the power of story with a deep understanding of human motivation and a disarming vulnerability that renders his essays at once profoundly wise and yet universally accessible. Mike's gift is his ability to convey transformative universal truths through authentic stories that connect with readers through shared emotional experiences. Readers who want to benefit from the wisdom of contemporary philosophy along with the joy and fun of personal reflection will love this book."
— **Eric Severson,** senior vice president of
Global Talent Solutions for Gap Inc.

"Nothing Changes Until You Do is a sweet and wise book written by a sweet and wise man. Full of refreshing insight and gentle wisdom, this book reveals its secrets as Mike reveals his compassionate humanity. Easy to read, easy to relate to, and easy to inspire."
— **Frederic Luskin, Ph.D.,** author of *Forgive for Good* and director of the Stanford Forgiveness Project

"Mike Robbins is a coach of the first order. If you're looking for an honest, down-to-earth, and practical approach to bring out what is best inside yourself, read *Nothing Changes Until You Do*—you won't be disappointed!"
— **Tim Ryan,** U.S. Congressman from Ohio
and author of *A Mindful Nation*

"Mike Robbins is amazing! The stories and ideas contained in the pages of this beautiful book are infused with authenticity and awareness. Reading this book is a gift for your soul."
— **Lynne Twist,** co-founder of the
Pachamama Alliance and author of *The Soul of Money*

"Mike Robbins is the real deal. He's honest and vulnerable, courageous and wise. He writes about real life, his personal highs and lows. By sharing himself so openly, he brings us back to ourselves, to our own life, and to what really matters most."
— **Robert Holden,** author of *Shift Happens!* and *Loveability*

"Mike Robbins is a gifted storyteller. The stories, ideas, and insights he shares in *Nothing Changes Until You Do* are important and impactful. Like when he has come in to speak to my team at Google, Mike's wisdom is beneficial in both business and in life."

—**Alan Moss,** vice president of U.S. sales for Google

"With stirring prose and focus, Mike Robbins will empower you with the latest wisdom on self-compassion and kindness. Read *Nothing Changes Until You Do*. It will change your life and the lives of the people around you."

—**Dacher Keltner, Ph.D.,** professor of psychology at UC Berkeley and author of *Born to Be Good*

"Mike Robbins is a great author, speaker, and friend. We have known each other for more than 20 years and I've seen firsthand the ways he has inspired me and others. Whether it is motivating my staff and players or being a living example of positivism, he continues to be an influence in my life. *Nothing Changes Until You Do* is a wonderful book that will inspire you to live a life full of perspective!"

—**AJ Hinch,** vice president, assistant general manager of the San Diego Padres

"Mike Robbins has taken a unique and enlightening approach to self-compassion in *Nothing Changes Until You Do*. Through vulnerable and inspiring stories he not only teaches us the importance of being kind to ourselves, but exemplifies it in the process."

—**Kristin Neff, Ph.D.,** *author of Self-Compassion*

"*Nothing Changes Until You Do* is a brilliant guide to the value of changing and exquisitely loving yourself through what life brings us. Mike Robbins's book is filled with fresh truths, shared vulnerabilities, and uncommon insights to open your heart and support you in the beauty of change and self-love."

—**SARK,** author, artist, succulent wild woman, PlanetSARK.com

NOTHING CHANGES *UNTIL* YOU DO

ALSO BY MIKE ROBBINS

Books

Be Yourself, Everyone Else Is Already Taken: Transform Your Life with the Power of Authenticity

Focus on the Good Stuff: The Power of Appreciation

CDs

The Power of Appreciation

NOTHING
CHANGES
UNTIL
YOU DO

*A Guide to
Self-Compassion
and Getting Out of
Your Own Way*

MIKE ROBBINS

HAY HOUSE, INC.
Carlsbad, California • New York City
London • Sydney • Johannesburg
Vancouver • Hong Kong • New Delhi

Published and distributed In the United States by: Hay House, Inc.: www.hayhouse.com® • *Published and distributed in Australia by:* Hay House Australia Pty. Ltd.: www.hayhouse.com.au • *Published and distributed in the United Kingdom by:* Hay House UK, Ltd.: www.hayhouse.co.uk • *Published and distributed in the Republic of South Africa by:* Hay House SA (Pty), Ltd.: www.hayhouse.co.za • *Distributed in Canada by:* Raincoast Books: www.raincoast.com • *Published in India by:* Hay House Publishers India: www.hayhouse.co.in

Cover design: Amy Rose Grigoriou • *Interior design:* Pamela Homan

Cataloging-in-Publication Data is on file at the Library of Congress

Hardcover ISBN: 978-1-4019-4455-1

17 16 15 14   4 3 2 1
1st edition, May 2014

Printed in the United States of America

SUSTAINABLE
FORESTRY
INITIATIVE

Certified Chain of Custody
Promoting Sustainable Forestry

www.sfiprogram.org
SFI-01268

SFI label applies to the text stock

CONTENTS

Introduction

This book is about one of the most important and challenging aspects of life—our relationship with ourselves. What I've noticed in my 40 years of living, especially in the past 13 as a coach, speaker, and author, is that it doesn't matter our level of success or the specific circumstances we face in life—the most essential human relationship we have is the one with ourselves. Sadly, many of us don't have a very healthy or empowering internal relationship and there seems to be an epidemic in our culture of self-criticism, self-doubt, and thinking that our inherent value is directly connected to what we do, the status of our relationships and family, the money we have, our appearance, or any other number of external factors. None of which is true.

The more unhealthy and critical our relationships are with ourselves, the more it manifests in various negative ways in our lives. We sabotage our success; turn to addictions of all sorts (food, work, alcohol, drugs, sex, technology, and so on); treat the people close to us in unkind ways; damage our bodies; and create drama, conflict, and suffering in many areas of our lives. These behaviors are inconsistent with self-compassion, self-acceptance, and self-love, which are the core themes of this book.

Making peace with ourselves is fundamental to everything that truly matters in life. When we genuinely feel good about who we are, and when we treat ourselves with kindness and love, everything flows from there. Regardless of how "good" or "bad" the circumstances or situations in our lives may be, our ability to deal, respond, succeed, and ultimately thrive has everything to do with how we relate to ourselves.

I've been speaking and writing about these important themes for over a decade, and I am passionate about them. They are also things that I have found (and continue to find) difficult in my own life. I subscribe to the philosophy of "we teach best what we most need to learn." In that spirit, I'll start by sharing some of my own journey, which led me to write this book specifically.

I haven't written a new book in five years. My first book, *Focus on the Good Stuff*, came out in 2007 and my second book, *Be Yourself, Everyone Else Is Already Taken*, in 2009. In the span of just three years, I wrote two books and my wife, Michelle, and I had two daughters (Samantha, who is now eight, and Rosie, who is now five). It was an incredible and exciting time for us in so many ways—filled with many of the things Michelle and I had dreamed about when we first got together. However, by the end of 2009, I felt exhausted and confused. As I reflected on the previous three years, in particular that year of 2009, I was disappointed, disheartened, and overwhelmed by life, work, and fatherhood. And most painful and insidious of all was that I felt awful about myself. Here I had all these things that I said I wanted, but I wasn't happy—in fact, I was pretty miserable.

Somewhere along the way I had lost touch with my passion, purpose, and inspiration. I had fallen into the traps of both survival and ego-edification. I was trying to keep up with the various demands and pressures of my expanded life and trying to prove to others (and myself) that I was good enough, worthy of attention and recognition, and legit as an author, speaker, coach, husband, father, and man.

That was a particularly rough year for both Michelle and me. Although we had a lot of "good" things going on (at least on the surface) and we expected it was going to be a monumental year of success and growth for us, it ended up being filled with disappointment, struggle, and definitely some growth (but not the kind we wanted). Due to a variety of factors, by the end of the year, we found ourselves $105,000 in debt and more than $300,000 upside down on our house (having "bought" a home we really couldn't afford, which we financed 100 percent, near the top of the market in an area that went down in value significantly when the housing bubble burst).

In addition, parenthood was kicking our butts big-time, and while we never expected it would be easy, we weren't prepared in any way for how relentless, all-consuming, and fundamentally life altering it would be. We love our girls deeply, but being parents was really hard at times, and it was taking a big toll on each of us individually, as well as on our marriage.

I had lost my way and was in a state of deep emotional pain and confusion—questioning just about everything about myself, my work, and my life. I'd gotten so caught up in trying to keep up, achieve, and produce that at some level I felt like I'd forgotten who I was and why I was doing the things I was doing in the first place.

That difficult year, as painful and humbling as it was, turned out to be a beautiful catalyst for growth, healing, and change. I remember saying to Michelle at one point toward the end of 2009, "What if we stop trying to *look* happy and successful, and actually focus on *being* happy and successful? I bet if we actually *are* happy and successful, we'll look like it, too."

Since then, life has taken some interesting, intense, and miraculous twists and turns. There've been some huge highs and some incredibly difficult lows, and I've learned an enormous amount—about myself, my work, my life, and the world around me.

Some of the most difficult challenges have been dealing with the death of my mom from lung cancer, our financial difficulties, and our two miscarriages. I've also had some deep and painful struggles with my own self-criticism and self-loathing—often focused on my appearance, as well as being constantly challenged by the competing demands of my business, my family, and my personal growth and desires. Sometimes I feel as though I'm letting down the most important people in my life, including myself, because I don't know where to focus my time and attention.

In addition to these painful experiences, which have been growth inducing and transformational in many ways, there have been some amazingly exciting and wonderful things that have manifested in my life during these years. We were able to do a short sale on our house and exit with integrity in a way that felt good and responsible to us, all things considered. Miraculously, within an 18-month period, we not only got out from underneath the mess of our house situation but also paid off our entire debt and set up a responsible, reality-based financial plan. Our girls have been thriving in their new school, and parenthood has gotten easier and more enjoyable. While it still kicks our butts all the time and Michelle and I sometimes look at one another as if to say *What were we thinking?* we're having more fun and doing things that create greater joy, adventure, and excitement for our girls and our family.

My speaking business has grown in wonderful ways, giving me the opportunity to travel around the country and the world, sharing my thoughts and ideas with some pretty cool clients like Google, the San Francisco Giants, Gap, Twitter, Charles Schwab, eBay, and many more. And, thanks to the success of my business, our continued commitment to our financial health and awareness, and the sale of my mom's house, not only have we remained debt-free, but we've been able to save and invest a significant amount of money (for the first time in our lives), as well as move into an amazing new house in a community that we love!

More important than any of these external successes and accomplishments is that I feel like I've been able to go deeper into myself, my growth, my healing, and my own transformation over the past few years. I've made my own self-care, personal growth, and spiritual connection more of a commitment in my life. I also feel like I've started to live and embody more of what I've been speaking and writing about over these past many years in terms of self-appreciation and self-love.

As I've gone through all of these twists and turns, and as I've continued to work with people from all different walks of life, I've been constantly reminded that everything comes back to our relationships with ourselves. And, no matter what it is we're facing, the most important and difficult aspect of it is always how we relate to ourselves.

If we can figure out a way to be authentically gentle, kind, and loving to ourselves as we attempt to do whatever it is we attempt to do, our chances of success and fulfillment increase dramatically. If we don't, it can make the smallest task, action, or desire seem like a mountain we can't even begin to climb. In other words, *Nothing Changes Until You Do*!

As excited as I am to be writing this book and sharing it with you, the scariest and most challenging part of it is dealing with that negative voice in my head, my gremlin (aka my inner critic), who constantly tells me all the reasons why I can't or shouldn't. This is how the gremlin works: It's critical. It's mean. It's judgmental. Its only goal is to convince us that we're small, weak, and unprepared. The gremlin, which is the voice of our negative ego, lies to us about who we really are and tries to hold us back. Unfortunately, we listen to and believe the gremlin too often.

This book is about how to take back your power from the insidious and negative impact of your gremlin and be gentle with yourself in the process. In the chapters that follow, I share stories from my own life and from the lives of others—with insights, questions, suggestions, and ideas about how you can be more kind, forgiving, and appreciative of who you are and how you are, right now. Not after you've figured it all out, lost some weight, made more money, found the right person, or somehow become the "perfect" version of yourself.

I've learned a lot through various experiences, and from many teachers, counselors, mentors, friends, and others. I have figured some things out and struggled to make sense of many other important aspects of life. My intention in writing this book is to share some of these experiences and insights with you in a way that can help you on your journey of growth, discovery, and fulfillment.

This book is designed to give you deeper insight into yourself and the most important aspects of your life—to help you get out of your own way, keep things in perspective, and focus on what truly matters to you. But most of all, it will help you to have more compassion, more acceptance, and more love for yourself— thus giving you access to more compassion, more acceptance, and more love for the people (and everything else) in your life.

While the stories in this book focus on me and people I know, the most important person in this book is you. Your relationship to yourself gives you the context for how you relate to everyone and everything around you. Unfortunately, most of the feedback you get about how to live your life comes from the expectations of others and/or of the culture or environment in which you live. And while these things and people are important and essential to life and growth, what's most essential is how you relate to and feel about yourself. Hopefully these stories will help you see your life in a new way.

I acknowledge you for picking up this book, which, in and of itself, is an act of self-love. I feel grateful, humbled, and honored to be embarking on this journey with you. Here we go . . .

CHAPTER 1

Focus on What Truly Matters

My mom, Lois Dempsey Robbins, was diagnosed with stage four lung cancer in early March of 2011. The disease spread very quickly and on June 13 of that same year, she passed away. I was with her through her dying process, and it was both horrible and beautiful at the same time.

It was difficult for me to see my mom's physical deterioration and how much pain she was in. I also struggled with the realization that she was going to die and that at 37 years old I would be without either of my parents (my dad died in 2001), and my girls would grow up without their grandma, who absolutely adored them.

However, there were some amazing moments as well. About a week before she died, my mom and I were sitting on her bed talking. She was already starting to fade in and out, but in a clear and lucid moment, she looked at me and said in a hushed tone, "I'm sorry I didn't teach you more, Mike." I was a bit surprised to hear her say this; my mom wasn't big on apologies or vulnerability, although in that final month or so she really softened and opened up in beautiful ways. "That's okay, Mom," I replied. "You taught me more than enough." After a pause I added, "Sorry I was such a pain in the ass sometimes." She looked at me and said, through a laugh, "It's okay; that's what you were supposed to do." We both laughed and cried a little, but mostly laughed. Our relationship had its challenges over the years, but in that moment, we connected in a very real way.

This type of closeness, and the family connection, deep conversations, healing, insights, love, forgiveness, and support were some of the most wonderful things I experienced in the days and weeks before and after her death.

My mom's diagnosis, illness, and passing caused me to look more deeply at the things and people in my life that matter most—as is often the case when we go through a traumatic event. Through this challenge, I was given perspective and awareness.

What I noticed is that, sadly, I don't focus on what and who truly matter to me as much as I'd like. I often get distracted by fears, ego-obsessions, drama (in my own life and in the world), ambitions, and all sorts of survival instincts and emotional reactions. While I understand that this is all part of being human, I also recognize that when I get distracted like this, I'm not able to fully engage in the most important parts of my life.

Why do we get so distracted? Why does it sometimes take illness, crisis, injury, tragedy, or even death to wake us up and get our attention?

I think we clutter up our lives with too much "stuff." We're so busy, overcommitted, and information-obsessed. Our never-ending to-do lists are long and we run around trying to "keep up" or "be important," and in the process stress ourselves out. Even though many of us, myself included, often complain that we can't do anything about this—based on the nature of life today, technology, or our responsibilities, families, and jobs—most of us have more of a say over our schedules than we admit. We can choose how much we engage in electronic communication or the amount of "stuff" we cram into our daily lives. Much of this distracts us from what's most important and keeps us from feeling our true emotions, which is one of the reasons we keep ourselves so busy and distracted in the first place.

It can be a little scary to focus on what truly matters. Some of the most important people, activities, and aspects of our lives may seem unimportant to those around us, and may or may not have anything to do with our careers or taking care of our families. Some of these may not even be things that other people like, understand, or agree with. Even if they are, sadly, it's often easier to just watch TV, check our e-mail, clean our house, plan our day, surf the Internet, and merely react to what's going on around us than to actively engage in the things we value most.

We also may not actually know what's most important to us, or we at least have some internal struggle about what should be. With so many conflicting beliefs, ideas, expectations, and agendas within and around us, it's not always easy to know with certainty what matters most to us. And, even if we do, it can take a good deal of strength to live in alignment with this on a regular basis. Whether it's our lack of clarity or our fear of letting other people down (or maybe a bit of both), focusing on what truly matters to us can be more tricky than it seems on the surface.

While these and other "reasons" make sense, not focusing on what matters most to us has a real and often negative impact on our lives, our work, and everyone around us. We end up living in a way that is out of synch with who we really are, which causes stress, dissatisfaction, and missed opportunities and experiences.

3

What if we did focus on what truly mattered all the time—not simply because we experience a wake-up call, crisis, or major life change, but because we choose to in a proactive way? What would your life look like if you let go of some of your biggest distractions, the often meaningless worries and stresses that take your attention, and actually put more focus on the people and things that are most important to you?

One of the most profound things my mom said before she died was, "I want people to know that they don't have to suffer through this." As the end was getting closer, my mom's desire to share her wisdom increased, and it was beautiful. Because I was more focused on what mattered and less distracted by my own busyness, worries, to-do list, and even my judgments, I was actually able to pay more attention to her and really listen to the wisdom she had to share, which was such a gift.

Here are some of the key lessons I learned from my mom as she began to surrender and open up in the final days of her life. These are simple (although not easy) reminders for each of us:

Express Yourself—Say what you have to say; don't hold things back. As my mom got closer to death, she began to express herself with a deeper level of authenticity and transparency. We had conversations about things we'd never talked about before and she opened up in ways that were both liberating and inspiring. Too often in life, we hold back because we're afraid of rejection, judgment, and alienation. Expressing ourselves is about letting go of our limiting filters and living life "out loud."

Forgive—My mom and I come from a long line of grudge holders. Like me, she could hold a grudge with the best of 'em. I watched as she began to consciously and unconsciously let go of her grudges and resentments, both big and small. It was as if she was saying, "Who cares?" When you only have a few months (or weeks) to live, the idea that "life's too short" becomes more than a bumper sticker; it's a reality. And, with this reality, the natural thing for us to do is to forgive those around us—and ourselves.

Live with Passion—Going for it, being bold, and living our lives with a genuine sense of passion is so important. However, it's easy to get caught up in our concerns or to worry what other people will think about us. My mom, who was a pretty passionate woman throughout her life, began to live with an even deeper level of passion, although her body was deteriorating. In her final days and weeks, she engaged everyone in conversation, talked about what she loved, shared grandiose ideas, and let go of many of her concerns about the opinions of others. It was amazing— such a great model and reminder of the importance of passion.

Share Your Appreciation—At one point, my mom said, "It's so important to appreciate people . . . I don't know why I haven't done more of that in my life." Even in the midst of all she was going through, she went out of her way to let people know what she appreciated about them—and people shared their appreciation with her as well. My friend Janae set up a "joy line" for people to call and leave voice messages for my mom in her final days. We got close to 50 of the most beautiful messages, all expressing love and appreciation for my mom—most of which we were able to play for her before she passed away. Appreciation is the greatest gift we can give to others, and we don't have to wait until we're dying to do it or until someone else is dying to let them know!

Surrender While my mom clearly wasn't happy about dying, something happened about a month and a half before she died that was truly remarkable—she surrendered. For my mom, who had a very strong will and was a fighter by nature, this probably wasn't easy. However, watching her surrender to what was happening and embrace the process of dying was truly inspirational and life altering for those of us around her—and for her as well. So much of the beauty, healing, and transformation that occurred for her and for us during her dying process was a function of surrendering. Not giving up, giving in, or selling out, but making peace with what is and choosing to embrace life (and in this case death) as it shows up. Our ability to surrender in life is directly related to the amount of peace and fulfillment we experience.

My mom taught me and all of us that even in the face of death, it's possible to experience joy—what a gift and a great lesson and legacy to leave behind. We don't have to wait until painful things happen in our lives to wake us up—we can practice observing what we're paying attention to and asking ourselves the simple but important question, *Does this truly matter?*

CHAPTER 2

Remember that a Bad Day for the Ego Is a Good Day for the Soul

A while back I was listening to a radio interview with Michael Bernard Beckwith, founder of the Agape International Spiritual Center and author of *Life Visioning*, and he said, "A bad day for the ego is a good day for the soul." When I heard this, I laughed out loud. The wisdom of his statement resonated with me deeply. I thought about a number of experiences in my life that have been quite "bad" for my ego (i.e., embarrassing, disappointing, and even painful) but in hindsight have been great for my own growth and development (i.e., my soul).

One of the most painful and powerful examples of this was when my professional baseball career ended. I was 23 years old, in my third season in the minor leagues with the Kansas City Royals, when I injured my pitching arm. The injury led to a series of surgeries and ultimately the end of my playing career. Among the many lessons I learned from that experience, the most important had to do with appreciating myself, my talent, and my experience while it was happening, not after the fact. I spent most of my time while playing baseball all of those years (especially in college at

Stanford and in the minor leagues) thinking I wasn't good enough. I compared myself to everyone around me and held my breath hoping that I didn't mess anything up. And, when it was all said and done and I hadn't made it to the major leagues due to my injury, I thought, *Oops, I think I missed the point.*

This lesson has been a key motivator in my life and with my work, which is why I've written and spoken about it as much as I have all these years. However, a few years ago, I had an experience with my daughter, Samantha, that deepened the wisdom and insight from this lesson in a new way. It was April of 2010 and Samantha was four. She had the week off from preschool for spring break, and I decided to take the afternoon off so I could take her to see Cal and Stanford play an afternoon baseball game in Berkeley, not far from where we live. Her baby sister, Rosie, who was one and a half at the time, stayed home with Michelle. Given the nature of our lives, my schedule, and us still figuring out how to manage with two young kids, this was precious one-on-one time for Samantha and me, and we were both very excited about it. As we were driving to the game, Samantha, who was sitting in her booster seat behind me, asked, "Daddy, are you going to play in the game?"

The previous fall, Samantha had seen me play in our annual alumni game down at Stanford—an exhibition game between the current Stanford baseball team and any of us former players who are able to show up and courageous enough to get back out there on the field and play against the college kids. Anyway, Samantha had seen me in my uniform and since we were now going to see Stanford play, she wanted to know if I was going to.

"No," I said.

"Why not?" asked Samantha.

"Daddy doesn't play baseball anymore," I replied.

"Yes you do," Samantha said. "I saw you."

"Oh, honey, that wasn't a *real* game," I said.

"I don't understand," said Samantha.

"Sweetie," I said. "Daddy doesn't play baseball anymore because I hurt my pitching arm and had a bunch of surgeries on it, which caused me to stop playing."

"You mean you *can't* play baseball anymore?" Samantha asked.

"That's right, sweetie," I said.

"Are you sad about that, Daddy?" she asked.

"Wow, honey, I appreciate you asking me that," I said. "No, I'm not sad. I was when it happened; it was a pretty big deal, and I was very upset. However, that was a long time ago and I'm not sad about it anymore. In fact, I'm grateful."

"Grateful?" Samantha asked, quite surprised and confused. Even at four years old, she knew what it meant to be grateful for something since we talk about gratitude a lot at our house. "Why are you grateful that you can't play baseball anymore, Daddy? I don't understand."

"Well, honey," I said, "if Daddy hadn't hurt his arm, I never would've met Mommy . . . and I wouldn't be your daddy." Then, I burst into tears!

"Daddy, are you okay?" Samantha asked.

"I'm fine, sweetie, just fine," I said, as I wiped the tears from my eyes. I was shocked by how emotional I got in that moment—it hit me at a deeper level than ever before.

Too often our desire to protect our ego—to avoid failure and embarrassment—causes us to sell out on ourselves, not go for what we truly want, or hold back in a variety of detrimental ways. When we remember that even if things don't turn out the way we think we want them to, not only will we survive, we can grow in the process. As Randy Pausch said in *The Last Lecture*, "Experience is what you get when you didn't get what you wanted."

This is not to say that the *only* way to grow in life is through suffering, disappointment, or pain. However, when we do experience difficulties, we have the capacity to turn these "bad" things into incredible opportunities for healing and transformation. While it may not seem that way to us (or our ego) initially, the deeper part of who we are (our soul) knows that everything happens for a reason and that there are important lessons in every experience.

Think of some of the things that have happened in your life that seemed awful to you at the time but in hindsight are things you're incredibly grateful for.

The most elegant, pleasurable, and self-loving way for us to grow and evolve is through joy, success, and gratitude. However, due to the fact that difficulties do occur in life and that we often give away our power to the "bad" stuff (through resistance, judgment, or worry), learning to relate to our challenges in a more positive and conscious way is a crucial part of our growth.

Remembering that our ego is usually what's at risk when we're scared can remind us that we don't have nearly as much to lose as we think we do. Embodying this insight— that a bad day for our ego is a good day for our soul—with empathy and perspective allows us to live with a deeper sense of trust and openness.

CHAPTER 3

Nothing Changes Until You Do

A while back my counselor Eleanor said something simple but profound to me: "Nothing changes until you do." She went on to say, "Mike, you keep trying to control and manipulate the situations, relationships, and outcomes in your life—thinking that if they changed in the way you want them to, you'd then change and things would be better. It actually works the other way around."

The truth of Eleanor's feedback resonated deeply with me when she first said it and, of course, inspired the title of this book. She continues to remind me of this all the time, which I appreciate, as it helps me catch myself when I focus too much of my attention on changing the world around me instead of focusing on the only thing I can really change—me.

I've had a number of important examples of an internal change resulting in an external/tangible change in my own life. One of the most significant times this happened was when I got the contract for my first book, *Focus on the Good Stuff*, in 2006. From the time I was in college, I had dreamed of writing a book. In those days, it was more of a fantasy than an actual goal. But after my baseball career ended, after my short stint in the dot-com world was over, and I started my speaking and coaching business, this fantasy became a dream that I wanted to make come true.

Writing and publishing a book now felt like a big, but also practical, goal given my new business and career path. Thanks to some great help and mentoring over the next couple years, by mid-2003 I had a full book proposal and a literary agent, which was quite a big deal for me—especially given my age at the time (29) and my fear of writing.

My agent started submitting the proposal for my book, which at the time, we were calling *The Power of Appreciation,* to various publishers in New York. The first round of submissions went out to ten different publishers, all of whom rejected it. The second round of submissions, which we sent out a few months later after some tweaks and adjustments, went out to seven more publishers; again, all rejections. By the end of 2003, I was feeling pretty disappointed and disheartened. The following year, my agent and I parted ways, and I didn't think my dream of becoming an author was anywhere close to coming true.

In 2005, I decided to take another crack at it. I got a new agent, made a few more tweaks to the proposal, and changed the title to *Focus on the Good Stuff.* And, at the beginning of 2006, we were ready to start submitting the updated proposal. After seven more submissions and seven more rejections, I hit what felt like my rejection limit.

In late February, my new agent said to me, "Mike, you're a nice guy, and this appreciation message is a good one, but I'm not sure it's going to happen." I trusted my agent and took her feedback to heart, but that same night something just snapped in me. I got angry and had a big realization, so the next day I called her back and said, "Listen, I realized after our conversation yesterday that I've been waiting for permission from you, from these publishers, or from some outside authority to tell me that I'm ready to be an author and that this book is worthy of being published. I've decided that I'm not waiting for permission anymore. I've been scared to write this book and haven't been sure if I could even do it, but I'm ready now, and if no publisher wants it, that's fine; I'll just publish it myself."

My agent said, "Okay, I hear you. Before you do that, there are three more publishers on my list. I will send it out to them and see if there's any interest. But, if they're not interested, I don't know what else to tell you." She sent the proposal out and within just a few days she got back to me and said, "Guess what? All three are interested!" And within a few weeks, I had a contract in place to write and publish my first book!

Although I had made some changes, the proposal was essentially the same one that had been rejected 25 other times total and 7 times within the previous month. There really wasn't anything different with the book idea itself; something had just changed within me. I shifted and was finally ready, which, at the deepest level, is what I believe allowed it to happen.

In hindsight, I can see that it happened at just the right time, when I was actually ready—mentally, emotionally, and practically. It seemed like it took a very long time, from 2001 when I first started working on the proposal, to 2006 when I finally got the contract. And, even though those five years were filled with a lot of rejection and doubt, the manifestation of this specific goal was less about all of the practical things that were involved in making it happen and more about my internal shift and change—once I was truly ready, it happened.

We've all had this experience in our lives in both big and small ways. Do you ever notice that when you're having a bad day or a rough time in life, even the people and activities you normally love don't bring you the same amount of joy? On the flip side, when you're having a great day or things are going really well in life, even the people or circumstances that might normally annoy you somehow seem much less stressful. In those simple situations, your perspective and your own internal state have a big impact on how you experience life, not the other way around.

What if we put more attention on our own growth, evolution, and transformation—and less attention on trying to change the people and circumstances around us? This doesn't mean that we'd stop caring about what other people do or say. It also doesn't mean we wouldn't give feedback to or make requests of those around us. We also wouldn't stop working toward specific changes, goals, and dreams related to the most important aspects of our lives.

However, by letting go of our insatiable desire to fix, change, and control everyone and everything around us, we give ourselves the space to focus our attention on the true source of our own happiness, success, and fulfillment—ourselves!

CHAPTER 4

Remember that You're Valuable Just Because You're You

A few years back, I started playing a game with my girls, Samantha (our eight year old) and Rosie (our five year old). The game goes like this: I ask them, "How much does Daddy love you?" They respond by putting one or both of their arms up into the air as high as they can and say, "This much."

I say, "That's right!"

And then, I ask them a very important question, "And how come Daddy loves you so much?"

To which they say, "Because I'm me!"

I then say, "That's right, just because you're you!"

It's a fun, sweet, and powerful game that I love playing with them, and it's something I hope to continue for many years. I play this game as much for them as I do for myself. For the girls, I want them to know that my love and appreciation for them is not based on what they do, how they look, how well they listen, if they come in first place in the swim meet, if their teacher has good things to say about them in school, or any other conditions, expectations, and accomplishments.

For me, I do it for two main reasons. First of all, as a father, I find it challenging at times to keep my heart open and to stay connected to my love for my girls when they do or say things that upset me. This game serves as a reminder that my intention is to love them unconditionally—even in those moments when I don't approve of what they're doing. This is often easier said than done—especially when my girls do or say things that I deem disrespectful, ungrateful, or worst of all, mean. The challenge for me is to stay connected to my commitment of unconditional love and at the same time give them feedback, boundaries, and consequences that will serve them well. This is, by far, one of the greatest challenges of parenthood for me.

On another level, by saying this to my girls on a regular basis, I feel like I'm healing something deep within me that I've carried around for most of my life—the belief that my value as a human being is based on certain conditional, material, or external factors (accomplishments, appearance, approval of others, status, and so on). Even though I know better than to use these external factors as a basis for my self-worth and value, I find it challenging at times to let go of the conditioning and feedback I've received from the outside world.

How about you? How much of your own worth do you place in the hands of other people's opinions, material success, or other outside factors? If you're anything like me, and many of the people I know and work with, probably quite a bit—or at least more than is healthy. The belief that we have to do specific things, produce certain results, look a particular way, and so on, in order to be valuable or lovable causes a great deal of suffering in our lives. From an early age, most of us have been doing whatever we can to gain approval and love from those around us. It starts with our parents, siblings, and family members when we're very young. As children and adolescents, it extends to our teachers, coaches, and especially our friends. As we move into adulthood, it continues to expand to include our colleagues, clients, and anyone we deem important to our success in life.

At the age of seven, I started playing baseball (well, T-ball, actually) and I loved it. Not only was it a fun game, but I was really good at it—which made it even more fun. For a young, sensitive boy who struggled with deep feelings of insecurity and whose father was not only absent, but also beginning what would become a six-year odyssey of mental hospitals, halfway houses, suicide attempts, noncommunication, and more as he struggled with serious bipolar disorder, baseball became a safe haven for me. It was a place where I received approval, recognition, and love—or at least what felt like love to me as a boy and adolescent. From the age of seven all the way until I decided to walk away from the game on my 25th birthday (after four surgeries on my pitching arm), I had a love–hate relationship with baseball. I loved the game itself and had enjoyed lots of wonderful experiences playing. However, since my identity was so wrapped up in it and the approval, recognition, and "love" I received from playing were so conditional, I got to a point where I resented this great game.

While there's nothing inherently wrong with our desire to have the respect and admiration of those around us or to accomplish our most important goals, we often give away our power, consciously or unconsciously, to the people, circumstances, and results (or lack thereof) in our lives.

Our true value has nothing to do with any of these external factors. At the deepest level, we're valuable as human beings just because we're us—not because of what we do, how we look, what people think of us, or what we produce or accomplish.

In my very first session with my counselor Eleanor a few years ago, she explained to me that part of what caused the suffering and insecurity in my life was when I looked outside myself to fulfill my needs, which, by the way, she said was true for most human beings. She then explained a unique set of seven needs that was, as she described it, a modified version of Maslow's hierarchy of needs:

1. Safety

2. Security

3. Belonging/Value

4. Love

5. Knowing

6. Beauty

7. Spirituality

Eleanor then taught me a simple but powerful meditative technique to use as a way of learning to fulfill my own needs.[1]

I have used this technique a lot over the last few years and it's had an incredible impact on my life. It has been a great reminder and a practice for me to focus on fulfilling

[1] Specific instructions for how to do this meditative technique, as well as a link to the page on my website where you can download a free audio recording of me guiding you through it verbally, are listed in the appendix section of the book on page 203.

my own needs—not erroneously expecting people, accomplishments, circumstances, or situations outside of myself to do it for me. The bottom line is that we are safe, secure, valued, loved, known, beautiful, and spiritually connected—just because we are who we are. That's it. We can't earn or lose that which is inherently ours.

CHAPTER 5

Be Gentle with Yourself

In April of 2009, my book *Be Yourself, Everyone Else Is Already Taken* came out. The book was released on a Monday, and we had a big launch event at a local hotel. The following few days consisted of the online launch campaign, some media appearances, and a few other events—exciting stuff. Toward the end of the week, I was finally able to get to the local Barnes and Noble near where we were living. I hadn't been in an actual bookstore since the book had come out.

I wanted to check out this particular store because my publisher told me that not only were they carrying the book, but they would be featuring it up front the first month it was out. I was excited about that. When I walked into the store, at first I didn't see my book, which concerned me. But before I went over to ask someone where it was, I saw it out of the corner of my eye. In the middle of the store, they had a big circular display for the new releases, and there was a small stack of my books there, on the back side of this display.

I walked over, picked up a copy, and stood there, admiring my own book. Although I had boxes of them in my office, seeing it in the store for the first time filled me with a sense of pride and enthusiasm. Then I had this thought: *Should I buy one?* I know this might sound a bit narcissistic and self-absorbed, and it is. But what I'd learned when my first book came out is that books are essentially on consignment in the stores. This means that if nobody buys them, they get sent back to the publisher. A few of my fellow author friends and mentors had told me that it was totally okay, especially in the first few weeks after it comes out, to pick up a few copies of your own book when you're in a store, to "help the cause," so to speak. I had done this a few times when my first book came out, but for some reason I felt more self-conscious about it this time around.

As I stood there in the middle of the Barnes and Noble, I debated for a while in my head and finally decided, *The heck with it. I'm going to do it again, but just one copy.* I took the book and got in line. As I was standing there, I told myself that when I got up to the front, I would let the person behind the counter know that it was my book and it had just come out that week. The closer I got, the more nervous I began to feel. When it was my turn to pay, I put the book down on the counter and the woman at the cash register immediately said, "We've been selling a lot of these."

"Really?" I asked excitedly.

Then she asked me a question that kind of threw me off: "Did you see this guy on TV or something?"

Although her question made sense since I had done a few local TV interviews that week, it totally caught me off guard, and here's what I said in response: "Ah, no, ah, he's a local author. I just want to support him." As it was coming out of my mouth, I was thinking, *What is that?*

I don't know if this has ever happened to you, but I was mortified by what I'd just said. The woman behind the counter had no idea it was my book, although she probably thought something was up, given my awkward response and the strange look that I'm sure I had on my face. I couldn't even figure out how to recover or say anything else. All I could do was reach into my wallet and pull out my credit card, with *my name* on it, to pay for the book. With my head down, I signed the receipt as fast as possible, grabbed the bag containing my new book, and literally ran out of the store. Standing there on the street corner, I thought, *I wrote a book on authenticity, and I just* lied *to that woman.*

The irony of this experience was not lost on me, and I found myself laughing about it once the shock and embarrassment of the moment passed. I told Michelle about it right after it happened and ended up telling the whole story to a group of people I spoke to about the book a few days later. It really seemed to resonate with them and also made them laugh. Being able to talk about it, laugh about it, and share it with others is actually one of the ways I was able to be gentle with myself. I could have been overly harsh and critical of myself for what I had done and said at the Barnes and Noble, but I chose not to be. This has now become one of the key stories I tell when talking about the challenges of being authentic and the funny, paradoxical (or even hypocritical) nature of being human.

Essential to our ability to grow, evolve, and change is our capacity to notice what we do and to make conscious adjustments. However, the best way for us to do this is to have compassion for ourselves. All too often we either stay in denial about certain things that are detrimental to us, or when we do notice them we end up judging ourselves so harshly that we hurt ourselves even more in the process— thus making authentic change difficult, painful, and elusive.

My friend Karen Drucker, an amazing singer, songwriter, author, and speaker, has a beautiful song called "Gentle with Myself," which is one of my absolute favorites; it inspired the title of this chapter. This song, which is all about self-compassion, has a few poignant lyrics that I love. It starts with, "I will be gentle with myself, and I will hold myself like a newborn baby child." Imagine if we held ourselves in that way—with the kind of love we offer to a newborn. Whether pertaining to something we're trying to accomplish, an important relationship, our physical body, a challenge we're facing, or anything else—we often tend to be hypercritical of ourselves, which never helps.

Later in the song, there is a lyric that I sing to myself all the time, especially when I'm feeling scared, resistant, or worried about making a change, taking a risk, or going for something I want—"I will only go as fast as the slowest part of me feels safe to go." This is such an important message, although often counterintuitive for those of us who pride ourselves on pushing past our limits and being bold. While taking bold actions and going for it in life are things I do believe are important and valuable, sometimes the best thing we can do is slow down, have patience, and give ourselves permission to feel scared. When we do this in an authentic and loving way, the fear almost always subsides, and then we can motivate ourselves, take action, or make any change we want—from a place of truth and self-compassion. When we're gentle with ourselves, we remember that treating ourselves with kindness, acceptance, and love is essential to our growth and our well-being.

CHAPTER 6

Ask for Help

A question I love to ask when I'm speaking to an audience is "How many of you like helping other people?" No matter where I am in the world, how big the group is, or the type of people I'm speaking to (business executives, parents, athletes, salespeople, small-business owners, teens, personal-growth seekers, or anyone else), just about every single person will raise their hand in the affirmative to say "Yes, I like helping people." I then ask a second question: "How many of you *love* asking other people for help?" On average, only about 10 percent of the hands will go up in response to this one.

It's an interesting human paradox that most of us enjoy helping others but very few of us feel comfortable asking for help. We erroneously think that asking for help makes us weak, needy, or inferior. We worry that people will judge us, reject us, or disappoint us. However, when we have the courage to ask for help, while we may not always get exactly what we ask for, we give ourselves a chance to get the support we need. We also give other people the opportunity to do something important, sacred, and meaningful—support another human being in need, which almost everyone loves to do.

One of the most profound experiences of support that I received in my life came from my father back when I was in college. In the middle of my junior year at Stanford, I got severely, clinically depressed. I was quite familiar with depression due to my dad's significant struggles with bipolar disorder, as well as the many other members of my family who suffered from various forms of mental illness. When I got diagnosed with clinical depression at the age of 20, not only was it incredibly painful and scary, it was also coupled with the fear and dread of having now "caught" what my relatives referred to as "the family curse."

In the midst of this intensely difficult experience, I realized that I needed help. And although my relationship with my dad had improved over the previous few years, it still wasn't the type where I reached out to him for support. Quite frankly, at that point in my life, I didn't know if I trusted him or felt safe enough with him to ask for his help. But, given what was going on, it felt like my dad might actually be uniquely qualified and well suited to support me.

So I decided to call him. When he answered, I said, "Dad, I could really use your support. Can you come down and see me?"

He didn't own a car or have a whole lot of money at that point, so I understood that this wouldn't be super easy for him. But he rented a car that afternoon, drove down to Palo Alto, and showed up at my apartment that night. "What do you want to do, Mike?" he asked when he got there.

"I don't know, Dad," I said. "I don't really care."

"Let's go out to dinner and just talk," he said.

We sat at dinner, and my dad, who was usually a pretty big talker (which runs in our family), mostly just listened. I shared with him how I was feeling—scared, lost, sad, and hopeless. Without even saying anything, I could tell he knew exactly how I felt—I could see it in his eyes and feel it in his touch as he held my hand.

After a long pause in our conversation, he asked me, "Mike, have you ever heard the 'Footprints in the Sand' poem by Mary Stevenson?"

"No," I said.

"Well," he said, "I can't remember the whole thing word for word, but basically it goes like this, 'I had a dream that I was walking along the beach with God. Many scenes from my life flashed across the sky. In each scene I noticed footprints in the sand. Sometimes there were two sets and other times just one. This bothered me because I noticed that during the hard periods of my life, when I was suffering most, I could see only one set of footprints. So I said to God, "You promised me you would walk with me. But I've noticed that during the most difficult times in my life there has only been one set of footprints in the sand. Why, when I most needed you, were you not there for me?" Then God replied by saying, "The times when you saw only one set of footprints was when I carried you." ' "

I had never heard this poem, and it really touched me, especially given what was going on in my life at that specific moment. I sat there holding my dad's hand, looking into his eyes, and crying. For one of the first times in my life, I had the experience of my father carrying me—just like in that beautiful poem. I felt loved. I felt seen. I felt supported.

Thinking back on it now, I imagine it was a pretty profound and important moment for my dad as well. Although I'm sure he was concerned about me, it probably also felt good to him to be able to support me, especially with everything that had gone down in our past and how few opportunities he'd been given to show up for me like that.

Thankfully, due to a great deal of love, support, and help from my dad, my family, my friends; some good therapy and medication; and an amazing counselor named Chris (who I still work with), I came out of that depression. In hindsight, I can see that that experience was actually a pivotal moment in my life and my growth. I'm eternally grateful for even the pain of the depression, as it actually forced me to my knees and gave me almost no choice but to reach out for help.

Unfortunately, it often takes something incredibly painful for us to finally get over our own fear and resistance in order to ask for the help we need. What if we allowed ourselves more permission to ask for help?

There are a few important things for us to remember about asking other people for help. First, there's a difference between a *request* and a *demand*. A request is when we ask for what we want, without attachment. This means that we give the other person the freedom to say yes or no, and there is no consequence either way (i.e., we won't hold it against them, get all upset or self-righteous, or take it personally if they say no, even if we are disappointed). Sometimes, once we get over our resistance to asking for help, we actually make demands instead of requests. In other words, they *better* say yes, or they will be in trouble with us.

Second, it's important that we actually allow ourselves to receive the support. As much resistance as we have to asking for help, sometimes we have even more resistance to receiving it when it shows up. The easier we are to support, the more support we'll receive. For some of us, myself included, receiving support from others can make us feel scared, vulnerable, and even awkward. We worry that we're not actually worthy of support, that we'll owe the giver something, or that somehow we're inferior to the people who help us. None of this is true; it's just another negative ego trap.

Third, we need to remember the paradox of getting feedback and help from others: while it can benefit us greatly, at the deepest level, the answers, support, and guidance we are seeking are actually inside of us, always. The rub is that we often forget, and the support of those outside of us is a great reminder that helps us tap into our inner wisdom. When we embrace this important paradox, it actually gives us more freedom to ask for and receive support while also giving it to ourselves in a healthy and empowering way.

CHAPTER 7

Don't Get Caught in the Trap of Comparison

A few years ago a woman sent me an e-mail suggesting that I check out the website of another author/speaker. She said he reminded her of me and thought we should know each other. I looked at his site and was very impressed by him and his work. In addition, I quickly found that I was unconsciously comparing myself to him. My gremlin started telling me how much better this guy was than me. *Look at him, he's a stud: funny, good-looking, and savvy. His site is way cooler than mine, his approach is more hip, and he has this whole thing figured out much better than I do.* After looking at his website for just a few minutes and listening to my gremlin, I found that I was feeling jealous, inferior, self-conscious, and deflated.

Sadly, many of us spend and waste a lot of time and energy comparing ourselves to others in this way. Feeling jealous is a natural human emotion. And it's pretty common—especially given the nature of how most of us were raised and the competitive culture in which we live. However, comparison can have a negative impact on us, our dreams, our relationships, and many of the things we hold most sacred.

Our personal and cultural obsession with competition and comparison isn't new, although it seems to have intensified in the past few years with the explosion of social media, and how we share everything with one another in such a public way. I personally enjoy being able to celebrate the exciting stuff happening in other people's lives, and being able to share some of my own "good stuff" with others as well. At the same time, it can be a bit of a double-edged sword. While I'm often inspired by and excited about the success of others, especially those closest to me, depending on how I'm feeling about myself at any given moment, I can get easily triggered by their success and end up feeling insecure in comparison to them—especially if they accomplish something I'm still striving for.

On the flip side, I've noticed that this forum can also inspire bragging or feeling a sense of superiority when something goes really well in my life. This is even harder to admit and confront. And while it may seem like the opposite of insecurity, it's actually just the other side of the same coin. Heads, we feel superior, tails, we feel inferior. Both are detrimental to our growth and ultimately our sense of peace, fulfillment, and joy in life. This is a negative ego trap—and there are no true winners in this game. As Mark Twain said, "Comparison is the death of joy."

Growing up as a competitive athlete, I got lots of early experience and training about how to compete against others and try to beat them. This wasn't just about the other team; often the biggest and most intense competition was with my friends and fellow teammates.

On our baseball team at Stanford, there were almost 40 players on the total roster, 18 of whom were pitchers like me. When we'd travel to play games against other teams in our conference, only 22 guys were allowed to go on the trip and be on the active roster. Eight of these guys were pitchers. During a weekend three-game series, there were three starting pitchers, and usually only two or three of the relief pitchers would get a chance to pitch, depending on how the games unfolded. This meant that about half of the team and more than half of all the pitchers didn't even get to make the trip, let alone get a chance to play in the games. Needless to say, it created a pretty stressful and internally competitive environment. Some of my teammates were very close friends of mine whom I cared a lot about. Yet, at the same time, we were competing for a limited number of spots—like a cruel and very public game of musical chairs that we all wanted to win.

Whether it was in baseball, school, or other areas of life, I often found myself directly or indirectly competing in a pretty intense way with those around me when I was younger.

Although I've worked through and outgrown certain aspects of my intense competitive and comparative tendencies (and it's been more than 15 years since I played baseball competitively), I still find myself threatened by the success of others, at times—as if we're competing against one another for a limited number of "spots" or as if their success takes something away from me, which, in just about every case, it doesn't.

It's important to understand, however, that there is both negative and positive competition. Negative competition, which most of us are more familiar with, is based on two limiting and negative notions: First is the black-and-white idea of "us against them"—when we win, we're good, and when we lose, we're bad. Second is the stressful and damaging concept of scarcity—that there's a finite amount of success to go around, and if someone else succeeds, it takes away from us. Based on these notions, the goal is to beat anyone and everyone around us or, at the very least, avoid losing, and get as much as we can before someone else does. Sadly, this type of negative competition is everywhere in our culture and has been ingrained In how we operate in life, business, and even personal relationships. We have to be mindful of our own tendencies, and of our cultural programming, so as not to fall into this negative trap.

Positive competition, on the other hand, is about challenging ourselves, pushing our limits, and allowing the talent, skill, and support of others to help take us to the next level. When we compete in this conscious way, it's beautiful, important, and healthy—and has nothing to do with our true value as human beings. In other words, we aren't better or worse based on how we perform.

A simple example of this is with physical exercise. When we work out with another person, or with a group of people, we usually get more out of it. Why is this? Because we're challenged and held accountable, which forces us to show up, go beyond our perceived limits, and not quit (even if we want to). The competitive aspect of this remains positive and healthy as long as we simply allow ourselves to be pushed without looking for a particular outcome. It can turn negative if we allow our egos to take over and place value on who lifts more weight, who runs faster, or who "wins."

Of course, there are times in life and in business when we will "win" and times when we will "lose" based on whatever "game" we're playing and however we're measuring our results. And while there is a real impact to the results that we produce, living life as if it's a competition with everyone around us is a recipe for disaster.

When we're willing to let go of the ideas and decisions we made as kids and teenagers about who we are, and what makes us successful or valuable, we can step into a healthier version of competition that can truly empower and inspire us. It can help us move to new heights and depths in our relationships, our work, and our lives. Getting caught in the negative trap of comparison, while common and understandable, is a choice we make; it isn't something we have to do. When we're willing to notice our comparative tendencies, we can consciously choose to disengage in negative competition, and, more important, choose to appreciate and value ourselves in an authentic way.

CHAPTER 8

Be Real, Not Right

A few years ago, I delivered a seminar for a group at a technology company in Silicon Valley. After my talk, one of the participants told me privately a bit about what was going on with his team and asked if I would be open to speaking to his manager. His hope was that I could come in and help them address and resolve some of the issues they were having with trust and communication. I said yes, so he set up a phone call for me and his manager. When we spoke, the manager confirmed everything his employee had said, and we set a date for me to come back in and talk to his team.

When I walked into the conference room with this group a few weeks later, I was taken aback. While there were just eight people sitting around a table, the tension in that room was palpable. Have you ever walked into a room where you could just feel the bad vibes and animosity right away? That's how it felt in there; it was pretty intense.

They wanted me to give a talk on teamwork, communication, and trust. I was more than happy to do that, since I love talking about these important topics. However, while they seemed somewhat interested in what I had to say, about 20 minutes into my speech the level of tension in the room finally got too distracting. So I stopped, looked at everybody, and said, "Listen, I can keep talking about various aspects of trust, teamwork, and communication, but I think what would be most useful is if we actually talked about what's going on with you guys as a team."

I went up to the whiteboard in the conference room and drew a picture of an iceberg, which is the metaphor I often use when talking about authenticity and trust. I said, "I think there are some things down here below the water-line that aren't being talked about. And, if you all are willing to express and expose some of what's down there, it might make a difference not only for this conversation we're having, but for each of you personally and for your team.

"There's an exercise we're going to do now, and I'll start. We're going to go around the table and each of us will have a few minutes to speak. When it's your turn, just repeat this phrase, 'If you really knew me, you'd know . . . ,' and then share anything you'd like to about what you're thinking; how you're feeling; or what you're not saying in this moment—you know, the stuff that's down below your waterline, so to speak. Then go a level deeper, using the phrase 'If you really, really knew me, you'd know . . .'

"I'll go first," I said. "If you really knew me, you'd know that I feel an enormous amount of tension in this room. I'm not even sure what it's about, but it feels visceral. I literally felt it the moment I walked into the room. If you really, really knew me, you'd know that I feel scared to have this conversation with you guys. On the one hand, I'm worried that you won't open up and talk about what's really going on, which could make this exercise and this whole session become quite useless, awkward, and uncomfortable. On the other hand, I feel even more scared you will open up and really talk about what's going on. If that happens, it's possible that whatever comes out might be so messy and difficult that I won't be able to help or support you in coming to a resolution, which may end up making things worse."

When I finished talking, I turned to the first person to my right at the table, who happened to be the manager. As he started talking, it was obvious he was uncomfortable. He fumbled through the first minute or so of what he was trying to say, becoming even more uncomfortable—his face turned red, there were long pauses, and he looked at me as if to say, "Do I really have to do this?" Then, all of a sudden after another long pause, he started to talk about his wife, his kids, and some challenges going on at home. As he started to talk about this personal stuff, something dramatically changed in the energy of that room (as is often the case when someone gets real).

He then said, "Look, you know I'm a pretty private guy. I don't like to talk about this kind of stuff at work. Doing this exercise is uncomfortable for me. But, I've got all this stressful stuff going on at home, then I come to work and things are so challenging here, not just with the work but due to the fact that we're not getting along, we're not communicating, and we don't seem to trust each other. I know we've gotten into a lot of arguments as a team, and I've gotten into it with a number of you one-on-one in my office. Even though I often act like it's your fault, and I'll admit that I do like to be right—who doesn't?—the truth is I feel like I'm failing as a leader. If you really, really knew me, you'd know that in all my years of being a manager, I've never had this kind of difficulty with any group I've worked with, and I don't really know what to do."

It was an amazing moment of realness and vulnerability for him and the entire team. His authentic expression gave everyone in the room permission to open up and get real themselves. As we went around the table, each of the other seven people on this team (all of whom happened to be men, by the way) really lowered their waterline and shared what was going on in their lives, how they were feeling about work and the team, and whatever else they wanted to say to each other. They got real in a vulnerable way.

When we finished the exercise, I looked at everyone in the group and said, "I want to acknowledge each of you for your courage and willingness to get real." Then I asked a simple but important question: "From this place where we are right now, what do we need to talk about, address, and resolve over these next few hours for you guys to feel safe to be yourselves with one another and work through your conflicts?"

We proceeded to have a conversation over the next few hours about the issues they had identified—not a theoretical discussion about authenticity, communication, and trust, but a real conversation about what was going on for them as individuals and as a group, and how they could be real and trust each other in a genuine way. It was beautiful.

They didn't miraculously transform from being a non-trusting, dysfunctional team with everyone protecting themselves into being a high-performing team where people felt total freedom to be themselves, speak their truth, and trust one another completely in the span of a few hours. However, what they had done gave them permission to be real with one another and themselves, which was incredibly valuable and empowering. In doing so, they cracked the door open to a deeper level of trust and communication, which made a big difference.

They still had some work to do to repair their relationships, resolve conflicts, and open up lines of communication in a sustainable way. So I stayed in touch with them over the next few months, and things did start to change positively as a result of our session and the real conversations that took place that day.

As I learned from this group and have learned from working with individuals, teams, and groups of all kinds over the past 13 years, righteousness is one of the most damaging energies in our world and realness is often the antidote. Not only is it impossible to be right all the time, it's exhausting, stressful, and no fun (for us or others). The great saying, "You can either be right or happy, not both," is so true!

Each member of that team had justifiable reasons to not be real with the people around them. Understandably, it didn't feel safe due to the lack of trust and the unresolved conflicts that existed in that environment. However, when they each took responsibility for their own part in creating the situation and got real about how they were feeling, something began to shift. In other words, they let go of being *right* about what was *wrong* with those around them and the situation, and they started to get *real* about what was true for them personally.

When we're willing to lower our waterline and get real, we can liberate ourselves from unnecessary and unhelpful self-protection, righteousness, and disconnection. Down below the waterline is where our truth lies and where real freedom exists.

CHAPTER 9

Love Yourself (and the Rest Will Follow)

When Michelle was pregnant with Samantha, I got lots of unsolicited advice about parenting, which is what often happens when you're about to have a baby, especially your first. I'm sure most people meant well, but it got to be a bit overwhelming since much of it made no sense to me. I didn't have any real context for what they were saying. I did, however, get some parenting advice from Chris Andersonn, an amazing personal and spiritual counselor, that had a profound impact on me.

Chris said, "Mike, when your daughter is born, you have two primary jobs. They're both important, but the second one is even more essential than the first. The first job is to teach her how to be in the world. This means you'll have to help her learn things like how to walk, talk, read, write, look both ways before she crosses the street, tie her shoes, ride her bike, and much more. As she gets older, you'll have to teach her how to drive a car, manage her money, make good decisions, and all kinds of practical things about how to successfully navigate life. Now, this is a really big job; it'll go on for many years, you'll probably screw it up a bunch of times, but it's what you sign up for as a parent. And, as big as this first job is, it's not nearly as important as your second job as her father. The most important job you have is to teach her how to authentically *love herself* as she grows up."

I was a bit surprised to hear Chris say this. It wasn't something I'd heard before, even with all the advice I'd been given in the past few months. But the truth of what he said resonated with me deeply. After a bit of a pause, I asked him, "How do I do that?"

"You love yourself, and let her see that," Chris said. "This isn't easy. Self-love takes real commitment, courage, and follow-through. But if you do, that's how you can best teach her to genuinely love herself."

This was and is great advice—not just for parenting but for life. However, as I've learned over the past 8 years as a father, and the past 40 years as a human being, understanding the concept of self-love is quite a bit different (and easier) than actually loving myself.

How do you feel about self-love? More important, how well do you love yourself? For most of us, loving ourselves is something we may know is important, but often we have difficulty actually doing so in an authentic way. Why is this? What makes loving ourselves so tricky?

First, we have a tendency to demand perfection and to be hypercritical of ourselves. Most people I know and work with, myself included, have some version of "I'm not good enough" that runs their lives. While we may be aware of this phenomenon, we're often unconscious about certain aspects of it—both how it manifests and the negative impact it can have.

About a year after Michelle and I started dating, I was talking to her about some things that were frustrating me. I began to really rail on myself in a negative way, although I wasn't fully aware of what I was doing. She stopped me and said, "Hey, don't talk about my boyfriend like that."

A bit surprised by her comment, I said, "What do you mean?"

Michelle said, "Listen, if someone else were talking about you in such a negative way, I'd be upset with them. Just because you're you, doesn't give you the right to talk about yourself like that. You're my boyfriend and I love you; it offends me to hear you say those negative things about yourself."

Michelle's feedback stopped me in my tracks and made me realize that my self-criticism had a negative impact not only on me but also on her (and anyone else who cared about me). When we're obsessed with self-criticism and perfection demands (i.e., holding ourselves to unrealistic expectations that we never can achieve), loving ourselves is difficult, if not impossible.

Second, we sometimes feel embarrassed, guilty, or even ashamed of loving ourselves. My friend Susan Ariel Rainbow Kennedy (aka SARK), an incredible artist and the best-selling author of many inspiring books, tells a great story in her TEDx talk entitled "Succulence is Power." In it, she talks about walking into an elevator in New York City and being "blinded by the radiance of a man" she saw. She said to him, "Wow, you have the best energy!"

He responded by saying, "Thank you, I'm so in love with myself."

Susan said, "I thought to myself, 'Can he *say* that?' Then I thought, 'Why am I not saying that?' "

We've somehow picked up along the way that loving ourselves is not okay—we think it's arrogant, narcissistic, self-absorbed, and something we shouldn't do (or at least shouldn't admit to doing out loud to others who might judge us for it).

And finally and probably most insidious is that we don't know *how* to love ourselves and are often either unwilling or uncomfortable admitting this to ourselves and to others. This fear and self-judgment keeps us stuck. We worry that we're doing something wrong or, even worse, that there's something wrong with us for not being able to sustain self-love in a genuine way.

Self-love is one of those things that often falls into the category of "you know." It's referred to in various ways and by many people, but often in the vague sense of "Well, just love yourself . . . you know." Unfortunately, we *don't* know, or at least we aren't quite sure what it looks like, feels like, and *is* like to love ourselves—especially in particular areas of our lives (usually the ones that are most painful and difficult for us). Simply hearing people say "just love yourself" doesn't seem to address the true depth, challenge, complexity, and importance of learning how to do it in an authentic and sustainable way.

Self-love is what we're all searching for. Sadly, we spend most of our time thinking that someone or something else can give us what only we can give ourselves. To be truly fulfilled in life, we have to find the love within us and give it to ourselves. No other person, material possession, or accomplishment can do it. It's up to us. Self-love, as Whitney Houston sang about in her 1986 megahit song, is the "Greatest Love of All."

So how can we start loving ourselves in a more conscious, real, and effective way?

It's important to remember that we actually know how to do it and it's in our DNA, even if we've forgotten. One of my favorite memories of both of my girls when they were toddlers (between about one and two years of age) was watching them see themselves in a mirror. At this stage in a child's development, they are usually beginning to walk, and they have the ability to recognize that the little person they see in the mirror is actually them; it's quite fascinating and adorable.

Rosie really loved this. We had full-length mirrors on the closet doors in our master bedroom, and when she was there, she would often get so excited to see herself. I would say, "Who's that in the mirror, Rosie?" She would then squeal with excitement. Then I'd say, "Rosie, kiss the baby!" She would run over to the mirror and start kissing herself with such authentic joy and love; it was beautiful to see. I'm sure some of it had to do with the positive reaction she got from us, but at some deep level, it also seemed as though Rosie was just expressing her natural and innate love for herself, without any of the cultural conditioning we learn as we get older. When was the last time you did that when you saw yourself in a full-length mirror?

It's also important for us to remove the conditions we place on our "love" for ourselves and to treat ourselves with an enormous amount of compassion. If we only "love" ourselves when we do "good" things, "succeed" in specific ways, or take care of ourselves in ways we deem important, it's not actually love; it's approval. While there's nothing wrong with us feeling good about ourselves in relation to these and other positive things, truly loving ourselves is an unconditional process—which means celebrating all of who we are, both our light side and our dark shadow self. By letting go of our conditions and loving ourselves unconditionally, like how we often love babies, animals, or others whom we have little or no specific expectations of, we can start to deepen our authentic love for ourselves.

Even if we're not exactly sure how to do it or it may feel a bit awkward at first, we can give ourselves permission to express love for ourselves in any and every way possible. It's less important what we do specifically and more important where it comes from (i.e., a genuine place within us that wants to experience love for ourselves).

There are lots of things we can do—both big and small—to practice loving ourselves. Speaking kindly about ourselves, taking compliments graciously, forgiving ourselves when we make mistakes, taking care of our health, having compassion for ourselves, honoring our emotions, pampering ourselves, celebrating our successes (and failures), appreciating our "flaws"—these are all simple (although not always easy) things we can do to practice self-love. We can also ask for help and look to others who seem to embody self-love in order to get support, guidance, and inspiration from them. Loving ourselves is a lifelong, never-ending practice.

Self-love is the starting point, not the endgame, of our conscious growth and development. When we put our attention on loving ourselves in an authentic way, everything in our lives that's important to us—our work, our relationships, our goals, and more—flows from there with a sense of ease, joy, and, most important, love.

And, when we truly love ourselves, most of what we worry about and even much of what we strive for in life become meaningless. We may still have some worries, and we'll definitely continue to have goals, dreams, and desires. However, from a place of true self-love, the fear behind our worries and the motivation for our goals dramatically changes from something we have to avoid or produce in order to be valued to something we're genuinely concerned about or really want to accomplish.

CHAPTER 10

Don't Take Yourself
Too Seriously

I have a tendency to take myself a bit too seriously at times, especially when I get stressed, irritated, or scared. I've noticed that sometimes these feelings not only make me less effective in dealing with a difficult situation, they actually cause the difficulty itself, or at the very least exacerbate it. I also find that in these moments of taking myself too seriously, it's easy for me to become self-important and to think that the weight of the world is on my shoulders (which is often a bit of an overreaction and almost never helpful). As my friend Theo and I like to say in jest to each other from time to time, "Do you have any idea how important I think I am?"

When we take ourselves less seriously, we're able to see the humor in situations, find the silver lining when things don't go the way we want them to, and navigate through the ups and downs of life a bit easier.

When I was up in Seattle for a speaking engagement a few years ago, I saw just how important finding humor is. I'd flown in the night before the event and was scheduled to speak early the next morning. When I got off the plane I was hungry, so I decided to grab a piece of pizza as I waited for my bag. A few months prior to this, I'd taken a bite out of a frozen strawberry and cracked my left front tooth, which had originally been damaged when I was playing baseball in high school. Due to the initial injury, coupled with the trauma of the frozen strawberry episode, I ended up having to get my front tooth removed, and I was in the process of having an implant (i.e., false tooth) constructed for my mouth. This process actually takes a number of months, and in the interim I was given a nonremovable temporary tooth so that I wasn't walking around with a big hole in the front of my mouth.

As you can imagine, this posed some challenges, both in terms of eating and in terms of self-confidence. I've long struggled with issues of insecurity related to my appearance, so all in all this tooth problem was pretty traumatic for me.

Anyway, there I was in the airport in Seattle eating my pizza and, although I'd learned how to maneuver my food around the temporary front tooth (since I couldn't really use it to bite with), I took a normal bite without thinking about it. The next thing I knew, I looked down and the tooth had fallen out of my mouth and into my left hand. Although it was a nice catch, I immediately panicked and thought, *Oh my God, it's 7 P.M. and I have to speak at 9 A.M. I'm in Seattle and I now have a missing front tooth. What the heck am I going to do?*

With the tooth in my pocket and my mouth shut tight, I got my bag and made my way to my hotel as fast as I could. I was pretty freaked out. Thankfully my dentist, Shaya, happens to be a friend of mine; we went to junior high school together and she's really cool. I was able to call her that night and tell her what happened. She told me not to worry and to put the tooth in some water to soak. After that, I needed to find a drugstore and call her back from there. Luckily there was one just around the corner from my hotel. I called Shaya back as I walked into the store with my heart racing. She directed me to find the aisle where there was denture adhesive and told me which one to pick out. I followed the instructions on the box and did what Shaya told me to do the following morning—basically stick the false tooth back into my mouth using the denture adhesive. While it wasn't something I'd ever done before (and never thought I'd do in my life), it seemed to work and looked okay, although it felt really weird and made me talk with a little lisp.

I took a few deep breaths, said a prayer, and made my way down to the hotel ballroom. As you can probably imagine, I was quite nervous as I stood up in front of hundreds of people to deliver my keynote speech that morning. Being nervous before and even during a speech wasn't new for me; however, being specifically worried that my tooth might fall out of my mouth or that I might spit it on someone in the front row was definitely a new and odd experience.

As I was speaking, I could hardly pay attention because I was so preoccupied with my tooth, how I sounded, and my fear of what might happen. So after about 20 minutes, I had the audience pair up with each other to discuss something related to what I was talking about—I often do this because it allows people to relate their own experiences to some key theme of my speech; it also gives me a moment to catch my breath. On that particular morning, I really needed a moment for myself. As I was watching everyone talk, I thought, *This situation is so ridiculous that it's funny. I hope my tooth doesn't fall out, but if it does, these people certainly won't forget me or my speech anytime soon. Plus it would make a great story.* I laughed to myself, gathered the group's attention, and went on.

While I decided not to let the audience know what was going on inside my mouth (and my head), I was able to embrace the ridiculousness of the situation and not take it so seriously. Thankfully, my tooth stayed in my mouth and the speech went well. I was able to make it back home and then back to my dentist's office the next day without too much humiliation. A few months later, I got my permanent implant, and, thankfully, I don't have to worry about my tooth coming out anymore.

There are clearly times in life and certain circumstances that are genuinely serious. However, far too often we add unnecessary stress, pressure, and negativity to situations with our attitude of "seriousness." One of the best things we can do is laugh—at ourselves, at the situation, or in general.

I got a call from Michelle a few years ago and she was laughing pretty loudly on the phone. She had a funny story about the girls she wanted to share with me, as she often does. This one was pretty good and quite poignant.

Samantha was four and a half at the time and Rosie was two. It was late summer and Michelle was just trying to run some errands and she had to take the girls along—not a big deal on the surface. But keep in mind that this involved a two-year-old. As anyone who has ever dealt with a two-year-old knows, even the simplest thing can become a major production, and that's just what was happening with Rosie. She was going through a phase where she did not want to get into her car seat.

Michelle got the girls dressed, out the door, and to the car that morning; however, when they got into the car, Rosie threw a big-time fit—screaming, yelling, flailing her arms and legs, and throwing her body on the floor of the car—all to avoid her car seat. These types of fits can be challenging to say the least, and when they happen out in public, there's an added level of embarrassment and helplessness that can kick in, which was happening for Michelle that morning. Even though Michelle had quite a bit of experience with this, she said she was incredibly ineffective that morning in dealing with Rosie, and she found herself getting more and more frustrated.

At that particular time, with Samantha being four and a half, we were starting to teach her certain things that were appropriate to her age. One of the things that Michelle had been talking to Samantha about just the day before was what to do in case of an emergency and how to get help if she or someone around her needed it. So Samantha was sitting there quietly in her booster seat. She had buckled herself in like a "big girl" and was waiting patiently as Mommy and Rosie struggled through this conflict. Samantha, sensing Michelle's frustration and escalating panic, decided she wanted to intervene and help out. She calmly turned and said, "Mommy, I can go inside and call 911 if you want." As soon as Michelle heard this, she burst out laughing. She said she could hardly control herself and thought she actually might pee her pants. In the midst of her laughter, she stopped paying attention to Rosie for a moment. Once she gathered herself and calmed down a bit, she turned around to find that Rosie had crawled into her car seat and was ready to be buckled in.

As Emily Saliers from the Indigo Girls said, "You have to laugh at yourself, because you'd cry your eyes out if you didn't."

Laughter is actually important on many levels. Clearly, it helps shift our perspective and alter our mood, but research shows that it also has quite a positive impact on our physiology—relaxing our muscles, boosting our immune systems, releasing endorphins and decreasing stress hormones, and increasing blood flow to the heart.

I'm not advocating that we laugh ourselves into denial or avoid dealing with the serious aspects of our lives—as we all know, sometimes laughter can be used as a way of deflecting, or in other unhealthy and harmful ways. However, being able to bring lightness, levity, and laughter into our lives and relationships in an authentic and healthy way is one of the best things we can do to take care of ourselves and keep things in perspective. Teeth will fall out, kids will throw fits, and all kinds of frustrating things (both big and small) will occur in your life—find the humor in the situation and your outlook will change.

CHAPTER 11

Remember How Strong You Are

In early March of 2011, I was sitting in my car in the parking lot of the Ritz Carlton Hotel in Half Moon Bay, California, where I was scheduled to speak later that morning. Although it was a pretty big event, I wasn't feeling all that nervous about it—I had other things on my mind. I called one of my best friends, Theo, to reach out for his support. Theo and I have been friends for more than a decade—we've helped each other through a lot of big life stuff, even though we live on opposites sides of the country and due to our busy schedules don't actually get to see each other in person all that much. I love, trust, and admire Theo a great deal—not only is he one of the smartest people I know, he's also one of those people you can call at 3 A.M. and know he'll be there for you.

That particular morning the conversation focused completely on me and our house situation. We'd been trying to work with our lender to figure out how to get out from under the enormous negative equity position we were in. Things were really up in the air with the bank, doing a short sale wasn't looking all that good, and the reality that we might simply need to walk away and have them foreclose on us was a real possibility. I felt paralyzed by my fear, shame, and embarrassment, and I was completely overwhelmed by the circumstances.

I said, "I don't know if I can handle this. I can't believe we put ourselves in this situation. How could I have allowed this to happen? I feel like an idiot!"

Theo listened with empathy and understanding. Then he said, "First of all, Mike, stop being so hard on yourself. Yes, you've made some mistakes, but you're learning from them and you're clearly not an idiot. Second of all, even with the mistakes you've made, a lot of people are in your same situation. It's not your fault that the economy crashed and the housing market imploded. And, finally, it's important to remember that *you have more than this requires.*"

As I allowed what he said to resonate with me, I was touched by a few specific things. First of all, I was reminded once again why Theo has been a constant in my life. He's always able to acknowledge the reality of a situation and then put it in perspective. Second of all, his words made me stop and take inventory of some of the adversity I've overcome in my life. In so doing, I was reminded that I am actually quite resilient. I got to thinking more and more about my own internal strength (and the strength we each possess as human beings) over the hours and days that followed our conversation.

In just about every situation and circumstance in life, we really do have more than is required to not only deal with what's happening, but to thrive in the face of it. As the saying goes, *whatever doesn't kill you makes you stronger.* While I don't believe that we have to necessarily suffer and struggle in order to grow and evolve in life, one of the best things we can do when dealing with a major challenge is to look for the gifts and to find the gold in the situation as much as possible.

Each of us has overcome a lot in our lives—both big and small. If you spend enough time walking around the planet, chances are you'll experience some significant adversity. Dealing with and overcoming it not only teaches us a lot about ourselves, others, and life, but also gives us the opportunity to be reminded of our own power and strength. It's not that we won't feel scared, overwhelmed, angry, sad, embarrassed, confused, worried, or more—these feelings and many others are often a part of going through adverse times. However, remembering that "this, too, shall pass" will help us persevere in the midst of challenges, while reminding us that we can actually expand ourselves in the process.

One of the most painful yet growth-inducing experiences of my life was when I got my heart broken in my mid-20s. Sara and I met in college and started dating in our senior year. We were together for three and a half years, and had gotten pretty serious. Going through college graduation, the end of my baseball career, moving in together, the sudden death of her father, the start of our first jobs, a breakup and reconciliation two years into our relationship, and more had bonded us significantly.

In the fall of 1999, Sara decided she didn't want to be with me anymore, and we split up abruptly. I was crushed. I felt like someone had knocked the wind out of me. I'd never experienced emotions like this before in my life. It was hard to eat, sleep, and even get out of bed in the morning. I felt lost and worried I would never find my way again. At one point when I was deep in the throes of my despair, I remember having a vision that I was a running back in a football game. This was an odd vision for me, since I'd never played football. However, I saw myself running with the ball toward the end zone. There were a bunch of guys trying to tackle me, but I was holding on to the ball with both hands, driving my legs as hard as I could, and doing everything possible not to let them bring me down. This vision felt like a sign to me—that the pain, confusion, and loneliness were there for a reason. Although it was difficult, I was strong enough to withstand it, and if I continued to persevere, I would be okay.

While it did take some time, a lot of forgiveness, support, and inner work, I moved through that painful experience and gained a great deal in the process. I learned how strong I was, gained a deeper awareness and empathy for the experience of loss and heartbreak, and came away with a greater understanding of what's important to me in relationships and in life. Going through that heartache made me a better person and also helped get me ready to meet Michelle, which I'm eternally grateful for.

When we remember how strong we are, not only can it help us as we face challenges or adversity in the moment, it can give us much needed confidence and faith that we actually have what it takes to navigate this crazy and beautiful thing called life. As Glennon Melton, author of *Carry On, Warrior* and creator of one of my favorite blogs, *Momastery*, likes to say, "Life can be hard sometimes, but that's okay, because we can do hard things."

CHAPTER 12

Just Show Up

I gave my first paid motivational speech in March of 2001. The way it came about was somewhat serendipitous. The month before it happened, I attended my very first weekend workshop at the Coaches Training Institute (CTI) where I received my training as a professional coach. Prior to that first course, I got some new business cards printed up that said "Mike Robbins, Motivational Speaker." While technically this wasn't a lie since I had given motivational talks at a couple of high schools and Rotary Clubs, I hadn't been paid to give a speech. I wasn't what would be considered a "professional." These business cards were designed to be an "act as if it's already happening" type of thing for me. Since I didn't think I would know anyone at this workshop, I decided to pass out my cards and introduce myself as a motivational speaker—just to see how it felt.

The workshop went well, I learned a lot, and I met a number of great people including a woman named Christine, who worked for Sutter Health, a pretty big health care company with dozens of hospitals and medical centers throughout Northern California. Her job was in training and development, and part of what she did was bring in outside speakers and trainers to work with their employees. Christine and I hit it off and we exchanged business cards. She seemed like she'd be a good contact to have; I decided I'd reach out to her once I got my speaking business off the ground. The day after the workshop, I sent her a quick note to say how nice it was to meet her. I figured I'd circle back around with her in six months or a year.

Less than two weeks later, I got a frantic phone call from Christine. "Hey, Mike, it's Christine," she said, in a rushed manner. "Oh good, I'm so glad I caught you live on the phone," she continued. "I just got a call from the CEO at one of our large hospitals, Sutter Medical Center in Sacramento. He's all freaked out because he has a day-long management meeting next Wednesday, and his speaker just canceled. I told him, don't worry, I've got a great guy!" Christine then said, "So here's the deal: I gave him your number and he's going to call you in like twenty minutes, okay? Now, do me a favor and don't tell him that I've never seen you speak, because I told him you were *awesome*."

"Wow, Christine, thanks!" I said, not knowing exactly how to respond. I felt simultaneous joy and terror, not really sure which one came first—they were both there with lots of intensity. I wanted to say, *Thank you, but I'm totally not ready for this and am worried I'll screw it up,* but I didn't. I also wanted to come clean with her about my lack of experience, but I didn't want to blow the opportunity. In the midst of my conflicting thoughts and feelings, I simply said nothing. Christine said, "I have to get back into the meeting I just stepped out of to call you. Let me know how it goes with the call—he's a great guy, you'll love him and he'll love you."

We got off the phone, and the feelings of joy and terror continued, but the terror seemed to be taking over as the joy faded quickly. My biggest concern was that the CEO would ask a fairly basic and appropriate question like "Who else have you spoken for?" I didn't think my response of "Skyline High and the Mill Valley Rotary Club" was going to impress him very much. I figured once he found out I had almost no experience, there's no way he'd hire me, and not only would I miss out on this opportunity, I might damage my credibility and relationship with Christine. As I waited for the phone to ring, I made a commitment to myself that I was not going to lie to this man. But, if he didn't ask, I wasn't going to say anything.

He called less than 20 minutes later, and he never asked about where I'd spoken. As it turned out, he was a big baseball fan, so he was quite impressed with my sports background. We talked about baseball and teamwork—and some of the connections between sports and leadership. At the end of the conversation, he invited me to come up to Sacramento to deliver a 90-minute speech on "the keys to creating a championship team" for the 200 people attending his day-long management meeting. And, he actually offered to pay me real money to do this. I was stunned but found the courage to say, "Yes, I look forward to meeting you and speaking to your group." I got off the phone, let out an excited yell in my apartment, and then the feelings of terror hit me again, because, as you can imagine, I didn't have a 90-minute speech on "the keys to creating a championship team" prepared. But, over the next six days, I came up with one.

I made the two-hour drive from San Francisco the following week for the event. I was scheduled to speak at the end of the day, from 3:30 to 5:00 P.M.—probably not the most ideal time since people would likely be tired of sitting all day and ready to go home by then. I had turned 27 the month before, and when I walked into the room and looked around, I realized I was probably the youngest person there, which added to my already significant level of anxiety. By the time I got introduced to come up to speak, I was so nervous I could hardly even catch my breath. Have you ever felt so nervous that you were sure the people around you could actually hear your heart beating? That's how I felt.

I don't even remember what I said for the first ten minutes. It was like an out-of-body experience, and not the good kind. But soon enough, I started to calm down and have fun, and then things actually started to go pretty well. Toward the end of my presentation, I remember thinking, *I wonder if these people have any idea I've never done this before?* I was amazed that even in the midst of my fear and doubt, I actually felt pretty comfortable, confident, and natural up there. And, from the sounds of the applause and the positive comments afterward, it seemed like people resonated with me and my message, which felt great. It was definitely a peak experience for me, and I was proud of myself and grateful it had gone well.

As I was driving home still buzzing from the excitement of my speech, I asked myself a really simple but important question: *What did I just do that allowed that to work out so well, especially for my first time?* I came up with three answers to that question. First, I tried to just be myself, even as nervous as I was. Second, I tried to talk about things I know about and not pretend to know things I didn't. And finally, I tried to connect with the audience in a personal way. That was it.

Thirteen years later with now close to 2,000 presentations under my belt, those three things still ring true.

Too often in life, we unnecessarily overcomplicate things. As Woody Allen famously said, "Eighty percent of life is just showing up." I think he's right and that's true whether we're giving a speech, going out on a first date, having an important meeting at work, playing with our kids, trying something new, working on a creative project, or doing just about anything in life—big or small.

We erroneously think that we have to be prepared or organized in order to do certain things that matter to us. And while there is value in preparation and organization, for sure, often our obsession with these things is based on our fears or simply our inability to see that we're already prepared, even when we don't think we are. The most important thing we can do is show up and be ourselves.

CHAPTER 13

Give Yourself Permission to Make Mistakes

A few years ago, I was scheduled to fly to Dublin, Ireland, for a speaking engagement, and when I got to the airport I realized I'd forgotten my passport at home. I felt mortified and embarrassed—and then angry when I found out I wouldn't be able to get on my flight. After a few hours of stress and drama, I was able to get myself on another flight, which got me to Ireland in time for my event but cost me quite a bit of money and forced Michelle to have to drop what she was doing and rush to the airport with my passport.

As I was waiting for Michelle to arrive, my heart was racing and my mind was flooded with self-criticism. The conversation that my gremlin was having with me in my head went something like this: *You idiot! How could you be so stupid? Your passport was sitting right on your desk where it always is, and you just forgot it, for no reason. You're a flake! You get upset with Michelle when she forgets to itemize a receipt from Costco and here you make this ridiculous mistake which has now cost you $1,300 and caused unnecessary stress for her, the girls, and for you! You should be ashamed of yourself!*

No matter what I tried, I couldn't stop listening to my gremlin saying these horrible things to me. By the time

Michelle arrived at the airport, I was so upset with myself, when I came out to grab the passport from her at the curb, I cried in her arms. She was so kind, loving, and understanding in the midst of my anxiety, self-criticism, and embarrassment, I felt loved and supported by her in a beautiful way.

Even with the drama of the situation, I did realize that in the scheme of things, forgetting my passport wasn't a huge deal. However, it really upset me and caused me to reflect on how I react to mistakes—mine and other people's. What I realized is that I don't give myself or those close to me much permission to make mistakes. While mistakes aren't a huge issue in my life, I actually spend and waste a lot of time worrying about making them, and also find myself being unnecessarily critical of those around me when they make mistakes (both overtly and covertly).

Michelle's kind response to my mistake and the negative impact it had on her was a great model for how I want to be when someone around me makes a mistake—helpful, loving, and accepting. It also reminded me that having empathy and compassion for myself when I make a mistake is a much healthier and more positive way to deal with it. Sadly, my stress and self-criticism in response to the whole passport debacle took a toll on me—I didn't sleep much on my flights over to Ireland, and by the time I arrived, I was actually physically sick. It was a painful way to learn a very important lesson.

How do you relate to yourself and others when mistakes are made? While it often depends on the nature of the mistake (some are bigger than others, of course), many of us tend to be hypercritical with ourselves and those around us when it comes to errors. And the stress we associate with mistakes can actually make a difficult situation even worse.

Our fear, resistance, and self-judgment when it comes to making mistakes can also keep us from learning and experiencing new things. Children are great reminders of this. My girls have taught me so much in this regard. Over the past few years, watching my girls learn how to ride their bikes, swim, and ski has been a wonderful and inspiring experience. While these activities are fairly simple, they aren't all that easy to learn, especially at first, and they involve a lot of mistakes and failure in the process.

I didn't learn how to ski until I was 13, and although I enjoy it, it's not something I've ever been all that good at, which also means that it hasn't been a priority in my life. Michelle learned when she was five and used to go up to Lake Tahoe to ski a lot as a kid and as a teen. We went there for our very first ski trip together as a family in April of 2012. Samantha had just turned six and Rosie was three and a half. The plan was for Michelle and me to ski together, amazingly for the first time in our 11-year relationship at that point, and we were going to put the girls in ski school to see if they liked it. Michelle and I ended up having lots of fun, and the girls were troupers in ski school; neither of them absolutely loved it, but both of them were willing to try.

We decided to head back up to Tahoe the following January. This second trip went even better and the girls were starting to enjoy ski school—although the learning curve was still pretty steep and there was lots of falling down, failure, and mistakes involved for both of them. Samantha, now being almost seven, was picking it up a bit faster than her four-year-old sister, but they were both making progress. On the final day of our third ski trip, we took the girls out of ski school at the end of the day, and decided to see if we could ski down the mountain together. I think Michelle and I were more nervous about it than the girls were. We all got on the ski lift, which is one of the scariest parts of the whole thing, especially with young kids. Thankfully, the girls were fine and totally excited—in fact, they were giving us pointers about safe ways to get on and off the lift.

At the top of the hill, we got off the lift, adjusted all of our gear, and took a photo. It was a beautiful day at Squaw Valley in Lake Tahoe. And as soon as we were set, we started to make our way down the mountain as a family. It was amazing and exhilarating, but a little nerve-wracking as well. Incredibly, we made it all the way down, even little Rosie, and although there were some falls and stops along the way, there were no major issues and it was lots of fun!

As simple of an experience as this was, it blew me away. I felt inspired and proud of my girls, not so much for their skill as skiers but for their willingness to learn something new and potentially scary, and most specifically their willingness to make mistakes and fail, and still do it anyway.

What if we had more freedom to make mistakes and gave the people around us permission to mess things up as well? It's not that we'd start rooting for or expecting things to go wrong; we'd simply have more compassion and understanding when they did (which at some level is inevitable in life, family, relationships, and business).

By giving ourselves and others permission to make mistakes, we actually create an environment within our own being and within our key relationships and groups that is conducive to trust, connection, risk-taking, forgiveness, creativity, and genuine success.

While it can seem a little risky, and even counterintuitive, allowing more freedom for mistakes to be made creates the conditions for fewer errors to occur, and more fun, courage, and productivity to take place.

CHAPTER 14

Ask for What You Want

It was just another rainy Saturday afternoon in October of 2000 when I showed up at the Landmark Education office in San Francisco to visit a friend—but it turned out to be a day that would change my life forever. This was the day I met Michelle.

Landmark Education is an organization that delivers personal development seminars around the world. I'd been taking various courses and volunteering for them for the previous two years. When I walked into the office that day, Michelle happened to be volunteering. Although I came in to visit a friend of mine who worked there, I was much more interested in talking to Michelle once I met her. She was great—full of energy, passion, and enthusiasm, and she was adorable.

We chatted for a bit and I found out she was involved in Landmark's seven-month-long leadership training program, which I'd participated in the previous year. It sounded like she was enjoying the program but also finding it challenging (which had been my experience as well). It's pretty intense—both in terms of the time commitment and the personal growth involved. We sometimes referred to it as "transformational boot camp." Michelle and I shared a few stories about the program and a few laughs. I really wanted to ask her for her phone number or, more specifically, to ask her out. However, I was feeling a bit shy and insecure—I woke up feeling funky that morning and I didn't actually have a job at the time. I'd been laid off a few months earlier from the start-up where I was working (as were many of us 20-something, dot-commers) and had not yet found another job or gotten my speaking/coaching business started. Because of these things, I wasn't feeling abundantly confident about myself in that moment.

I spent the afternoon catching up with my friend and talking with Michelle whenever possible. I couldn't quite tell if she was flirting with me or just being friendly, and I didn't know what her relationship status was or if she had any interest in hanging out with me. The best (well, safest) idea I could come up with was to offer her some help with her homework from the leadership program.

As I was about to leave, I wrote down my contact information on a piece of paper (I didn't even have a business card at the time). I walked over to Michelle, handed her the paper, and said, "Here's my info. Feel free to get in touch with me if you need help with your homework." I was trying to make it seem like no big deal (although it was a big deal to me) and also trying to come across as confident (even though I didn't feel that way). She took the piece of paper, and simply said, "Thanks." Then, she reached into her purse and got out her business card holder. She said, "Here's my card," smiled, and handed it to me. I was fired up!

I left and figured I'd wait for a few days to call her, so I wouldn't seem too needy or pushy. The following Monday morning, I got up and went for a run. When I came back to my apartment, there was a message on my phone. It said, "Hey, Mike, this is Michelle. It was nice to meet you on Saturday. I wanted to see if you really meant what you said about helping me with my homework. I could use some help. Call me back and let me know."

I was excited that she'd called, and after hearing her message, I thought, *I really like this woman—she's confident, straightforward, and funny.* However, I also felt a little nervous because, while I was happy to help her with her homework, that wasn't really why I gave her my contact info. The truth was I wanted to ask her out, but I felt scared. *What should I do?* I thought. I contemplated it for about 20 or 30 minutes, and then said to myself, "You know what? I'm just going to tell the truth."

I picked up the phone to dial Michelle's number, with my heart racing and my hands shaking. When she answered, my heart raced even faster. I said in a pretend confident tone, "Michelle, hey there, it's Mike. Thanks for your message. Glad we met on Saturday. Listen, I'd be happy to help you with your homework, but to be honest, I was really just trying to find a way for us to exchange info so I could ask you out on a date."

There was a long pause on the other end of the phone. I held my breath. Then Michelle said with a laugh, "Oh good, I'd rather go out on a date anyway!" We went on our very first date the next week. And now, more than 13 years later, I'm glad I had the courage to simply tell the truth and ask for what I wanted—I'm also very happy that she wanted to go out with me! In hindsight, it would have been a lot easier if I had just asked her out when we met. It would have saved me a lot of unnecessary worry.

Unfortunately, we often tend to get in our own way, psych ourselves out, and allow our egos to run the show when it comes to asking for what we want. Whether it's in business or our personal relationships, we waste a lot of time trying to figure out the right way, the right time, and the right words to use in order to get what we want—instead of just authentically asking for it. Sadly, there are times when we simply don't ask due to our fear of rejection, disappointment, or embarrassment. While this is very common and we want to have compassion for ourselves in this process, all too often we give away our power to our fears.

My first job after my baseball career ended was in sales. I worked for an Internet company that represented hundreds of websites and sold advertising space on their behalf. The first week of my job, I had a meeting in my manager Steven's office. He had Scott, one of the executives from the New York office (where our company was headquartered), on the phone. Steven introduced me to Scott and asked Scott if he had any words of wisdom for me as a young guy just starting out in sales.

Scott asked, "Hey, Mike, how do you feel about hearing *no*?"

I wasn't sure how to answer the question, and could tell it was some kind of test. I said, somewhat timidly, "Ah, well, I don't really like it very much."

Scott said, "Well, it would be good to get over that! When someone says *no* to you, Mike, you should thank them." He continued, "First of all, because the more often you hear *no* the less scared of hearing it you'll become. And, second of all, every *no* gets you closer to a *yes*."

I appreciated Scott's wisdom, which not only helped me in my sales job, but is something I still think about today when I find myself scared to ask for what I want in business, my relationships, and life.

The more freedom and confidence we have to ask for what we want, without being pushy, demanding, or overly attached to the outcome, the more likely we are to get what we want. Can it be scary? Yes. Will we get disappointed sometimes? Of course. Might we feel rejected or embar-rassed from time to time? Yep. However, it's important to remember with both empathy and courage that, as one of my favorite sayings reminds us, "The answer's always *no* if you don't ask."

CHAPTER 15

Make Peace with Your Body and Appearance

I was in the bathroom one morning a number of years ago getting ready for my day. As I was shaving and taking care of my morning routine, my gremlin was actively and negatively commenting about a number of specific things related to my appearance. That nasty and critical voice in my head said, *Look at you, you look awful! Your hair is thinning, you're gaining weight, you have dark circles under your eyes, and those worry lines on your forehead keep getting deeper. You're clearly not taking good care of yourself.*

I was doing my best to ignore my gremlin, finish up in the bathroom, and get on with my day. As I was in the midst of this process, there was a series of loud bangs on the door—*boom, boom, boom*!

"Daddy!" said my then two-year-old Samantha. "Daddy, Daddy, Daddy—open up!"

Samantha, who has always been quite passionate, was going through a phase where she was barging into rooms, particularly the bathroom, all the time—so I'd been well trained to lock the door whenever I went in there.

"In a minute, honey. Daddy's shaving," I said.

Samantha continued to bang on the door and said, "Daddy, open the door! I have to tell you something *important*."

"I'll be out in a minute, sweetheart," I said, hoping she would just go away (although I knew there was little to no chance that would actually happen).

"Daddy," said Samantha, "it's *really* important."

I let out a big sigh, and with a towel wrapped around my waist, shaving cream on half my face, and a pretty bad attitude, I begrudgingly opened the door. "Yes, honey, what is it?" I asked, impatiently.

I looked down and saw Samantha standing there completely naked with a huge grin on her face. She looked up at me, spun around with a little twirl, and, with her arms outstretched, said, "Daddy, look how cute I am!" Then, quite pleased with herself, she gave me a big hug and ran off.

The irony of the situation was not lost on me. Although I wasn't sure if I should laugh or cry, it hit me in a profound way that Samantha's relationship to her own body and appearance was quite different and more empowering than mine.

Being hypercritical of my appearance, unfortunately, is a somewhat common experience for me and is something that I've struggled with significantly at times in my life. Some of the deepest pain and self-loathing I've ever felt has had to do with my feeling ugly and not good enough physically. I'm sure there are a variety of external factors that have contributed to this to some degree—growing up with parents who didn't feel good about themselves physically and who both talked about that quite a bit; being focused so intensely on the shape, size, and function of my physical body as a competitive athlete for almost 18 of my first 25 years on the planet; and being impacted by our media and culture, which seem to have an insatiable obsession with appearance, beauty, and body perfection. However, at the root of these issues for me (which I think is true for most of us who struggle with this) is a deep sense of feeling fundamentally flawed.

A couple of things have added to the complexity and confusion of this particular issue for me over the years. First is that I've gotten mostly positive feedback about my appearance. I've never really been significantly overweight. Nothing is physically "wrong" with me, but I still feel unattractive. Which leads to the second bit of added confusion: I'm a man. Body image stuff, as we often read about, is portrayed mostly as a "women's issue." However, it has been a major issue in *my* life. At times I'm not sure what's worse, feeling bad about my body and appearance, or feeling embarrassed that I feel bad about my body and appearance—both of these experiences have produced feelings of shame, guilt, sadness, anger, and conflict within me. And I know I'm not alone. This isn't something that only affects teens, celebrities, or women—it's something that people of all ages, body types, races, genders, backgrounds, and professions struggle with.

Most people I know have complaints about their bodies and how they look—whether they admit to them or not. There's nothing wrong with us wanting to look our best, take care of ourselves, and be fit. However, billions of dollars are spent each year by advertisers telling us we don't look good enough and need improvement. In return, we spend billions of our own dollars collectively on various products that are supposed to reverse our aging process, regrow our hair, smooth out our wrinkles, whiten our teeth, help us lose weight, make us look and feel better, and so much more. All in all, it sets up an unhealthy dynamic that is based on fear and scarcity. We buy into the idea that we have to do anything and everything we can to keep up, fight the natural aging process, and stay young, fit, and beautiful for as long as humanly possible. It can be exhausting and scary.

Over the past few years, I've started to get more real about my own struggles with my appearance and my deeper feelings about my body. Thanks to some great support, inner work, and healing, I've made good progress in this arena—although it still ebbs and flows for me and there is more work to be done. I had what felt like a pretty big breakthrough in 2012 when I decided I was finally ready, after a number of years of avoidance, to update the photos and videos on my website. My last photo shoot, which was in 2008, had been so upsetting and traumatic that I hadn't been interested in doing it again. But by 2012 the images and videos on my website were dated and it was becoming problematic.

My hair started thinning when I was in my late 20s. For someone who was already hypercritical of his appearance, this was a scary and painful development. In addition to my own body issues, hair loss had been a big thing in my family, as my father had lost his hair quite young and it caused him a great deal of pain and suffering. So in both my family and our culture at large, hair loss for men is seen as a very bad thing. Even though it's quite common, it's something people (especially other men) often comment on and make fun of. Losing your hair isn't really something you can hide or cover up all that well—it's out there for the whole world to see. By my early to mid-30s, it was becoming pretty obvious, and it was a source of deep pain, shame, and embarrassment for me. Most of the reason I hadn't gotten new photos taken had to do with my hair and my lack of acceptance about it. Although I'd been consistently shaving my head since mid-2011, something about getting these new photos and videos done made me feel vulnerable and scared in a way I wasn't sure I could handle.

I reached out to some of the people closest to me to ask for their support, and I found some good professionals to help with the photos and videos. Although I was pretty freaked out, I scheduled a photo shoot and also planned to take a look at some video footage of some speeches I'd recently given. The process of getting the photos taken and the videos filmed wasn't the hard part for me; it was looking at them afterward. Going into both the photo shoot and the speeches I knew were being filmed, I focused my attention on how I wanted to feel, not on how I wanted to look. I also did whatever I could to be kind and loving to myself, even though I was feeling self-conscious.

I had Michelle and also Melanie, who works with me, look at the photos before I did—so they could send me the ones they liked best (and hopefully get rid of some of the bad ones). That helped and I was actually quite pleasantly surprised by how they turned out. The videos, on the other hand, were more difficult, as I had to watch myself speaking for hours on end in order to pull out the clips for my speaking demo video and for various pages within my website. My gremlin had a field day with me at first, but after talking to my counselor Eleanor about it, she suggested that I focus on how I wanted to feel while I was watching the videos, which helped shift my perspective and made the viewing/editing process a little easier.

Although it wasn't my favorite thing in the world, the whole process ended up being a lot less painful than I expected and the net result was that I was able to launch a new website with updated photos and videos of myself, that fall—which was a huge deal for me on many levels.

As I contemplate future photo and video shoots, I still feel a bit scared and daunted. However, these feelings are less intense based not only on this past experience, but also on my personal commitment to making peace with my body and appearance. When I come from that place of peace, things are much different and more enjoyable than when I come from a place of criticism and judgment (i.e., the world of my gremlin).

What if we could befriend our bodies and not treat them like enemies we're trying to beat, conquer, or at least keep at bay? What if we could remember how accepting and celebratory we were about our bodies as young children? The key to all of this is not about losing more weight, finding the right workout program, getting the best products, or buying better clothes. It's really about us making peace with our bodies, and, on a deeper level, making peace with ourselves.

It's essential for us to forgive ourselves and to also forgive our bodies. In many cases, we have done, said, and thought really negative and damaging things to and about our bodies over the years. With a sense of healthy remorse and a deep sense of empathy, we can begin to forgive ourselves for how we've treated ourselves in the past. At the same time, we can practice forgiving our bodies for not being "perfect," which no body ever is or will be.

CHAPTER 16

Trust Your Gut

I was invited to speak a number of years ago at an event for a big insurance company. This meeting was an annual kick-off/goal-setting session held by the president of one of the four big divisions within this entire organization. Although there were only about a hundred people in the room (the senior-most leaders within this division), it was one of the highest-level and most important events I'd spoken at up to that point in my career. In addition, this was the first time I'd been hired by this client. Needless to say, it was a big gig for me, and I wanted it to go well.

The vice president of human resources, Christopher, who invited me to speak at the event, wanted me to talk about my book *Focus on the Good Stuff,* and specifically about how appreciation impacts employee morale, engagement, and productivity. He also made it clear to me that Bob, the president and his boss, was not a "touchy-feely" guy, so it was important to keep my presentation very business specific—using a lot of data, research, and information to make the business case for the value of appreciating employees.

I spoke with Bob on the phone prior to the event, and Christopher's assessment of him seemed quite accurate—he was a no-nonsense, bottom-line kind of guy. The call went well, and I was feeling excited about the opportunity to speak at this important meeting, although I was still feeling a bit nervous about it, too.

I was scheduled to speak for an hour at the very end of the meeting, but I asked if I could come a few hours earlier just to sit in the back of the room and get a sense of the group and meet some of the folks before I got up. As I was sitting in the back listening to Bob speak to his leadership team, he talked about the previous year, which had been rough for them results-wise, and about the new year, which he felt cautiously optimistic about. I could feel a lot of stress, pressure, and fatigue in the room—these people had been through a lot; they were worn out and worried about turning things around.

My gut feeling was, *These people need a good cry.* As soon as that thought would pop up, right behind it would be another one, probably from my gremlin, which said, *Shut up! There will be no crying today, Robbins, no touchy-feely stuff—remember what they told you. Stick to the script, do a good job, don't blow this. It could be a huge opportunity for you.* For the next few hours, as I sat in the back of that room preparing for my presentation, I continued to have this argument in my head between my intuition and my gremlin. It was, as you can imagine, a bit stressful and confusing.

When I finally got up to speak, I began talking all about the importance of appreciation, explaining the business case for it, citing some of the key research from the fields of positive psychology and strengths-based leadership in terms of engaging employees and maximizing results—all very important stuff. And though I understood this and saw that it was resonating with the group, my gut kept telling me that I needed to be talking in a more personal way.

One of my main intentions whenever and wherever I speak is to touch people's hearts and have an authentic conversation about not simply the topic at hand but also what's going on in the present moment and what we're all dealing with as human beings—both the joy and the pain of being alive. Although I felt nervous about it, I decided to trust my intuition. I had them pair up and do an exercise where they talked about some of the stress they were experiencing as well as what and whom they were grateful for—even in the midst of the uncertain times they were going through. The conversation shifted from data, information, and the importance of appreciation in business, to the relevance and importance of appreciation in life. As I closed my speech with a final, personal story, there was a lot of emotion in the room—a number of people were crying.

Bob, however, didn't look pleased. He had a pained expression on his face as he stood up to say a few closing comments to the group to end the meeting. Even though I felt good about the speech and could tell it resonated with the group, I sat there on pins and needles waiting to hear what Bob had to say. He started to tell a story about one of his mentors who had helped him through some difficult times and specifically over the course of the last year when things were really tough for him as a leader and for them as an organization. As he got to the end of his story, he paused, stumbled, and got choked up with emotion. By the reaction of the group, I could tell this wasn't common for him and was a pretty big deal.

As the meeting ended, Christopher made a beeline right over to me, grabbed me by the arm, and pulled me out into the hallway. He looked me straight in the eye and said, "Four years! For four years we've been waiting for him to show up like that as a leader . . . and, he finally did it today. Thank you."

Even though it was a risk and I felt scared, I chose to trust my gut and it paid off—not just for me, but for Bob and the entire group. Bob thanked me briefly that day and followed up with a heartfelt e-mail after the meeting. In his note, he talked about how important the message, meeting, and moment were to him personally and to his leadership group. I continue to work with this organization quite a bit and whenever I see Bob, he lovingly refers to me as "the guy who made me cry."

For most of us, myself included, trusting our gut can be challenging at times. We have a tendency to second-guess ourselves, to not listen to our intuition, to value the opinions of others over our own, or to hang on to negative memories from the past when we've made mistakes or "bad" decisions. These things make it difficult for us to trust ourselves and thus create issues in our relationships with others, our work, our lives, and, most specifically, in our relationships to ourselves.

How many times have you gotten an intuitive hit about something—positively or negatively—and not acted on it, and then regretted it afterward? This happens all the time in both small and big ways. We see an opportunity and want to step into it, but we hesitate, stop ourselves, or talk ourselves out of it—only to wish we would have been willing to take the risk, after it's too late. Or, we get a bad vibe about a person, situation, or project, and we don't do or say anything about it because we're afraid we might upset or offend someone, and then as things unfold, it ends up being a difficult or damaging situation for us and those around us. Again, in hindsight, we realize it wasn't a surprise at all; we just didn't trust our gut enough to speak up or do something early on. While this lack of self-trust is quite common and we don't want to judge ourselves for it in a harsh way, it's important for us to pay attention to it, as it can have a significant and often negative impact on our lives.

Trusting our gut is about choosing to listen to our intuition, taking risks, and letting go of always having to do things "right." When we trust our gut, we give ourselves permission to be guided by our inner wisdom. My tenth-grade physiology teacher, Mr. Young, used to always say to us while we were taking tests, "You think *long*, you think *wrong*." He would constantly remind us to trust our gut and go with our first answer, which was usually correct. We are often more aware, wise, and in touch with a deeper knowing than we give ourselves credit for. As we practice trusting ourselves at this level even more, our lives and everything important to us become easier, more abundant, and much more fun.

CHAPTER 17

Remember that It's Not the Circumstances, It's You

We took Samantha and Rosie to Disneyland for the first time a few years ago. Michelle and I hadn't been there for a long time and being back was a wonderful experience, reminding each of us of our childhood and lots of great memories. The girls loved it and we all had a blast—it was so much fun for us to experience the magic through their eyes.

I was struck, however, by the nature of many of the conversations that I overheard (mostly from other adults) during our trip. There were three primary themes of these conversations. First, people talked about how hot it was. We were there in August and it gets pretty warm in Anaheim, California, at that time of year. Second, people talked about how long the lines were. Again, the crowds tend to be pretty big in summertime at Disneyland. And third, people talked about how expensive it was. It's true; Disneyland is not cheap.

And this is called "the happiest place on earth"!

While none of these complaints seemed completely ridiculous to me, you would think that in the midst of a "fun" and "exciting" place like Disneyland, people would be happy. But

I quickly realized that this wasn't necessarily the case, and it brought back to mind one of my favorite Ben Franklin quotes: "Joy doesn't exist in the world, it exists in us."

The wisdom in Franklin's quote seems simple on the surface, but it's quite profound and a complete paradigm shift from how we tend to relate to the circumstances of our lives. Feeling like a victim of the things that happen to us is how we're taught to live. It's often encouraged by our culture, the people around us, and our own thoughts.

The circumstances of our lives, especially when they seem stressful or intense, do have an impact on us, for sure. However, all too often we give away our power—acting as though it's a foregone conclusion that we will feel a certain way based on specific circumstances or situations (e.g., the economy, our health, the weather, our family background, and so on). But our experience of life in any given moment is much more of a reflection of what's going on within us; it's not simply a reaction to what's going on around us.

A poignant and powerful example of this was Randy Pausch. Randy was a professor at Carnegie Mellon University in Pittsburgh, Pennsylvania. In September of 2007, he gave a lecture entitled "How to Achieve Your Childhood Dreams." It was part of a tradition at Carnegie Mellon called the "Last Lecture." The idea behind this was that as a professor, if you had one last lecture to give to your students before you died, what would you say? The "elephant in the room," as Randy talked about in his lecture, was the fact that it wasn't hypothetical for him because he was actually dying of pancreatic cancer and had been told that he had just months to live.

Randy, a 46-year-old father of three young children, gave his heartfelt, passionate, and inspiring lecture to about 400 people at Carnegie Mellon. Given the circumstances and the power of the lecture, it had a significant impact on everyone in the room. Because some people were not able to attend, the lecture was recorded and posted online internally at the university. Someone then posted it on YouTube, and it went viral. Ten million people watched the video in those first few weeks, and Randy was then invited on *The Oprah Winfrey Show* to reprise a portion of his lecture, which is where I first heard of him. He went on to write a bestselling book called *The Last Lecture* and inspired millions of people around the world before he ultimately lost his battle with cancer in July of 2008.

Like so many others, I was deeply touched and moved by Randy, his story, his lecture, his book, and his simple but profound wisdom. Most inspiring of all was how he approached his life, even in the face of difficult circumstances. At one point in the lecture, Randy says, "It's important to have fun; I'm dying and I'm still *choosing* to have fun."

Randy had justifiable reasons to feel sorry for himself, to be angry and depressed, and to feel victimized by his circumstances. However, he chose to approach his life and his death in a very different and inspiring way.

Most of us have had times in our lives when things were going great on the surface or we accomplished or experienced some wonderful external success, only to feel a sense of disappointment or sadness underneath because we didn't feel satisfied on a deeper level. And, on the other hand, many of us have had moments of incredible joy that weren't directly connected to anything "worthy" of these feelings externally. My girls have been teaching me about this from the time each of them started walking and talking. Pay attention to young children; it's amazing how the simple things bring them joy—like the wrapping paper or the box that a gift comes in when they're too young to even understand the present or holiday being celebrated.

Even though we know this dynamic to be true, we still seem to get caught in the hypnotic, erroneous notion that if we just got rid of some issues, altered some circumstances, manifested some increased success, or changed some specific situations in our lives, then we'd be happy.

Author and teacher Byron Katie says, "The definition of insanity is thinking that you need something you don't have. The mere fact that you exist right now without that which you think you need is proof that you don't need it."

What if we lived our lives with a deeper and more conscious awareness of the fact that we get to create our experience of life at any moment? Imagine what our lives, our careers, and our relationships would look like if we stopped blaming our experience on other people or on external circumstances. We would free up a great deal of positive energy and take back so much of our personal power.

This is about taking 100 percent responsibility for our experience of life. It doesn't mean that we can control everything, but it does mean that we make a commitment to live life by design, not default. It's also likely that we'll forget, slip up, and fall back into victimhood from time to time (or often)—we've been trained to live in "victim consciousness," even though it doesn't give us what we ultimately want. When we're conscious, willing, and courageous enough to live as the designers of our lives—we can literally transform our experience of life at any moment. Then, of course, we won't mind the heat, long lines, and expense of Disneyland (or anywhere else we are), and instead we'll enjoy the real magic of the experience. It really has less to do with where we are and what's going on, and more to do with us and what's happening internally anyway.

CHAPTER 18

Appreciate People

About ten years ago, I got an e-mail letting me know that there was a new *Chicken Soup for the Soul* book coming out called *Chicken Soup for the Single Parent's Soul*, and they were looking for submissions. As you probably know, this series of books has been around now for many years and there are hundreds of different Chicken Soup titles, which are made up of inspirational stories written by various people, focused on specific themes.

I'm a huge fan of these books and decided to write a story for this one called "Mom Taught Me to Play Baseball." Because my parents split up when I was three years old and my dad wasn't around a lot, my mom, who'd been a physical education teacher in the past, was the one who taught me how to throw and catch. She went to all my T-ball games, all my Little League games, all my youth league games, most of my high school games, and even many of my games in college when I was at Stanford. Once I got drafted and started playing professional baseball, my mom even flew out to visit me and see me play in the minor leagues.

The story that I wrote was an acknowledgment of her—everything she'd done, sacrificed, and contributed to me and my baseball career. I was pretty self-conscious about the story and my writing, because at that point in my life I wasn't doing much of it at all. It was before I'd published any of my own books and before I really even started writing articles or blog posts of any kind. Although it felt scary, I shared it with Michelle and she actually liked it.

I gathered the courage to submit the story, but didn't share it with my mom since I was still feeling quite nervous about it. After a few months, I hadn't heard anything from the Chicken Soup folks, so I just assumed it hadn't been selected. I figured they'd received a large number of submissions and mine simply didn't make the cut. Not long after I had resigned myself to the fact that it wouldn't be published, I got an e-mail saying, "Congratulations, we'd like to include your story in the book." I was thrilled!

I immediately told Michelle, who was equally excited. Then I said to her, "I've got to call my mom and tell her."

Michelle said, "Don't call her."

"What do you mean, 'don't call her'?" I asked.

She said, "What if you wait until the book comes out? You could surprise her."

"Wow, that's a great idea," I said.

We decided that in addition to not telling my mom, we weren't going to tell anyone, so we could ensure that the secret would stay safe. I sent an e-mail back to the woman at the publishing company who had contacted me, to find out when the book would come out. She got back to me and said it would be *14 months*. As excited as we were about the story, the book, and the secret, 14 months seemed like a *long* time. We weren't sure if we could make it that whole time without letting it slip, but amazingly we did. Over a year later, the book came out and no one close to me, especially my mom, had any idea my story about her was in there.

It came out in February, right around my birthday, and I got an advance copy. We were having dinner at our house to celebrate my birthday, just a few of us—my mom, sister, brother-in-law, and niece, in addition to Michelle and me. After dinner we went to sit in the living room because they had brought some presents for me. Once we sat down, I turned to my mom and I said, "Mom, before I open up my gifts, I actually have a present for you," and I handed her a copy of the book, which I'd wrapped.

She looked at me and at the gift with a puzzled expression. She said, "Honey, that's really nice, but it's your birthday. I'll open it later." Then she put it down. I hadn't expected this response and now she was messing with my plan.

I picked up the book, handed it back to her, and said, "Mom, I know it's my birthday, but do me a favor, just open it up."

At this point, I could tell she was getting a little uncomfortable and even frustrated with me, but she obliged and opened her present. Once she saw what it was, she said, "Thanks! How nice that they did one for single parents. Okay, I'll look through it when I get home." Then she put the book back down and looked at me as if to say, *Can we get on with your presents now?*

I picked it up again, handed it back to her, and said, "Mom, listen, I read this book and there's a story in here that really reminds me of you. In fact, I put a bookmark on the page where it starts, page 294. Would you do me a favor and read the story out loud to everyone?"

Now my mom was really uncomfortable, confused, and definitely annoyed with me. Somewhat begrudgingly, she grabbed the book, opened it up, and started to read the story, having no idea what it was or why I was asking her to do so. The first line of the story read, "'On June 1st, 1995, I was standing on the pitcher's mound at Rosenblatt Stadium in Omaha, Nebraska, about to throw my first pitch in the

College World Series.'" My mom looked up after reading that first line with a smile on her face and said, "This guy pitched in the College World Series!" totally not getting it.

Then she started to read the second line, and she stopped. She looked at me, then back at the book, then back at me again—you could tell her brain was working really hard. Then all of a sudden, her eyes got big and you could see that she finally got it—that the story was about *her*, and that I wrote it.

She dropped the book and started to cry. I reached over to pick it up off the floor. At this point I was crying, too. I handed the book back to her and said, "Hey, mom, if you don't mind, could you read the rest of it?"

And she did. My mom read that entire story out loud to all of us. It took her a little while, and it was quite emotional for both of us. It was a big deal for me, both personally and professionally, to have that story published. I was proud of it; it felt like a pretty big accomplishment, especially at that moment in my life. But the most meaningful aspect of it by far was being able to give it to my mom and to acknowledge her in that way. When we take the time and have the courage to let the people around us know how much we value them, it's not only a gift for them, it's a gift for us as well. That's how powerful it is when we express our appreciation for people—whether we do it in a big dramatic way or in a simple day-to-day way.

Appreciating another person doesn't mean that everything about them is perfect (no one is), or that our relationship with them is completely harmonious and free of conflict or issues. My mom and I had lots of challenges in our relationship throughout my life. But being able to acknowledge and appreciate my mom in that way was so meaningful for her and for me. And, now that she's gone, it has an even greater and deeper significance in my life and our relationship. Sadly, we sometimes wait until it's too late to let people know how much we appreciate them.

We have to be willing to look for and find things to appreciate about other people—which sometimes can be challenging, especially depending on who it is. Ironically, appreciation of others has less to do with them and more to do with us. We don't actually see people as *they* are; we see them as *we* are.

A number of years ago I was talking to a mentor of mine about some people in my life who were really bugging me at the time. After complaining about these individuals and explaining some of the details of the various conflicts for a few minutes, he asked me, "Hey, Mike, who's always at the scene of the crime?"

"What are you talking about?" I asked.

"Who is the common denominator in all of your relationships?" he asked.

"Oh," I said. "I guess that would be me."

"That's right," he said. "Everyone in your life is actually a mirror. When you change and you change the way you relate to people, the people around you actually change in your experience of them."

"So it really is all about me?" I asked, somewhat kidding and somewhat serious.

"Well, not in the ego-based, selfish way you might think. But in a real sense, yes, it is all about you."

Appreciating other people (or not) is actually just an extension and expression of us appreciating ourselves (or not). When we authentically appreciate ourselves, we give ourselves permission, perspective, and awareness to look for, find, and see the inherent beauty and value in other people. Once we see this, we can express it. When we have the courage to express our appreciation in a generous and genuine way, it can literally transform our lives.

As Wayne Dyer says, "When you change the way you look at things, the things you look at change." When we expand our capacity for appreciation of others and of life, what we're really doing is expanding our capacity to appreciate ourselves and, in so doing, we become more available for the love, connection, and fulfillment that we desire.

CHAPTER 19

Be Aware of the Imposter Syndrome

The day I arrived on campus at Stanford University as an incoming freshman was simultaneously one of the most exciting and humbling days of my life. Not only is Stanford one of the best colleges in the country, it also has one of the best baseball programs. Growing up as a kid who loved playing baseball and wanted to go to a great school, I'd long dreamed of going there. And I wasn't the only one who had this dream; there were literally tens of thousands of high school baseball players across the country who wanted a chance to play at Stanford. Fortunately, I'd done a good enough job on the field and in the classroom in high school that I got recruited and accepted. I'd actually gotten in during the early admittance period in November of my senior year, so by the time I showed up on campus, I'd been "the guy who was going to Stanford" for almost ten months.

But that very first day of freshman orientation, I had a simple but profound realization: *Oh yeah, everyone else here got into Stanford, too.* All of a sudden, I didn't feel so special, and my 18-year-old ego took a big hit. I was used to standing out both in school and in sports. Within a very short amount of time at Stanford, I realized that standing out here was going to be a lot harder. Not only did the idea of succeeding seem daunting to me, but as I began to get to know some of my fellow classmates and teammates, I started to wonder how I even got in. There were times, especially during that first year, when I worried that someone was going to find out I wasn't supposed to be there and they were literally going to ask me to leave.

This wasn't something that I talked about with anyone else. Most of the other kids in my dorm and the guys on my team seemed to be pretty confident and comfortable—they fit right in. I just assumed there must be something wrong with me and that I just wasn't as talented or sure of myself as everyone else. Of course, this wasn't actually true. Although I wasn't aware of it at that time, it turns out that just about everyone around me, especially given our age and where we were, felt some version of those same doubts. They were all just doing their best to pretend they didn't, as was I.

This is what's known as "the imposter syndrome." It's very common—not just with college kids at a place like Stanford, but for most of us, throughout our lives, and in various environments and situations. I see this with many of the people I coach, work with, and speak to. A few years ago I was delivering a day-long seminar to a group of senior leaders on communication and presentation skills. These folks were all very smart and accomplished, but like most human beings, they had some fear and difficulty when they got up to deliver a presentation. Public speaking is a place where the imposter syndrome shows up all the time. Most of us know that it's common for people to get nervous when they speak in front of a group and each of us has personally experienced the negative impact of our fear during a presentation. However, we often have these erroneous notions that we shouldn't be afraid because it means we're weak, incompetent, or unprepared. We also believe that somehow speaking is much worse for us than for other people—this false idea comes from comparing how we feel on the inside to how other people look on the outside, and they don't usually look as nervous as we feel.

As part of the seminar, I had each of these leaders deliver a presentation to their peers. They were filmed and received feedback from the group and coaching from me. It's an incredibly valuable experience and a rare opportunity, but can often be quite nerve-wracking, as you can imagine. A man named James got up and delivered his presentation, which went well from my perspective. I asked him when he was done how he thought it went.

"Terrible!" he responded.

"What makes you say that?" I asked.

"Well," James said, "first of all, I wasn't prepared; I forgot a bunch of things I had wanted to say, and I lost my train of thought a few times."

"Really," I said. "It didn't seem that way to me." Then I asked the group, "Did you guys think he was unprepared and off track?" All 12 people in the room unanimously said, "No!" I said, "James, I think you may be being a little overly critical of yourself; that was actually quite good and easy to follow. And, it's important to remember that no one knows what you were *planning* to say, they only know what you *actually* say."

James then said, "Second of all, I felt so nervous with that camera in the back of the room, all of you staring at me, and knowing I was going to be critiqued, that it was hard to concentrate."

"Wow, that's interesting, James. You didn't seem that nervous to me," I said. "On a scale from one to ten, with ten being the most nervous, how nervous did you feel?" I asked.

"About an eight," he said.

"How nervous did he look?" I asked the group. Most people said about one or two.

James's experience is quite common, not just with public speaking but life in general. We tend to be overly critical of ourselves, and often for no valid reason, which ends up either psyching us out or negatively impacting our experience—usually both.

I experience the imposter syndrome in my own life all the time—especially in my roles as a father, an author, and a speaker—where I'm often related to as an "expert" but don't always feel that way (and sometimes feel like the antithesis in certain situations). My girls are quite curious and like to ask a lot of questions, which is great, except when it's annoying, or, even worse, humbling. There are many times they ask me questions that I'm unable to answer—because I don't know the answer or because I want to protect them from something. And even though I sometimes want to say "Why the heck are you asking me that? How am I supposed to know?" I do my best to answer their questions as authentically and confidently as I can, and try to remind myself that I am actually qualified to be their father, whether I feel like it or not.

It's important to remember that everyone feels like an imposter at certain times and in certain situations. There's nothing wrong with us for feeling this way; it's just part of being human. And, if we can have compassion for ourselves when we feel like an imposter, two wonderful things can happen. For one thing, we can stop spending so much time and energy trying to hide or compensate for our insecurity (which makes life much more fun and less stressful). Also, we can remember that we *do* know some things, have certain skills, and might actually be qualified to be in the position or situation in which we find ourselves.

CHAPTER 20

Give Yourself Permission to Cry

Something extraordinary happened at Candlestick Park in San Francisco on January 14, 2012. Sure it was an amazing ending to an NFL play-off game between the San Francisco 49ers and the New Orleans Saints (which the 49ers won in dramatic fashion, making all of us fans here in the Bay Area very happy), but the monumental win wasn't what made it so remarkable to me.

As Vernon Davis, the tight end for the 49ers who caught the game-winning touchdown, came running off the field, tears were streaming down his face. He came to the sidelines and was embraced by his head coach, Jim Harbaugh, in a huge bear hug. Coach Harbaugh hugged him for quite a while and spoke into his ear in what I can only imagine was an expression of authentic appreciation and celebration. It was a beautiful and moving moment that transcended football, and even sports—it was about courageous triumph, raw human emotion, and vulnerable self-expression. (If you didn't get a chance to see this when it happened, I highly recommend searching for the video of it online; it's quite moving.)

Of course, I loved it—not just because I'm a huge sports fan and like to see my hometown teams win (especially after many years of not winning, which was the case for the 49ers that year in the play-offs), but because it highlighted something very important . . . the power of tears! I also loved it because you don't usually see a big, strong football player like Vernon Davis break down and cry in the arms of his coach in front of 65,000 fans in the stadium and millions of people watching on TV. But he did, and it was a powerful scene and an important reminder of what it means to be human.

One of the many things tears can do is remind us of our humanness, our vulnerability, and our connection to one another and to things much bigger than the specific circumstances we are facing. We cry for different reasons and based on different emotions. Sometimes we shed tears of pain, sorrow, anger, frustration, or grief. Other times, tears show up because of love, joy, inspiration, hope, or kindness. Regardless of the underlying emotions, crying often makes us feel better and is one of the most authentic expressions of emotion we experience as human beings.

However, many of us have a great deal of fear, resistance, and judgment about tears—both ours and those of other people. While this tends to vary based on our age, upbringing, gender, and the environment in which we find ourselves, I'm amazed at how often crying is seen in such a negative way in our culture, even today.

As a man, I was trained early in my life, like most of the men I know, that "boys don't cry." Based on this and a variety of other factors, I sometimes find it challenging to access and express my own tears. But I do actually love to cry, so when my tears show up, I let them flow, often quite passionately.

One of the places my tears often flow is on airplanes. I don't know why, but for some reason, being on airplanes gets me into a heightened emotional state. I was on a flight a few years ago and decided to purchase a movie on my personal TV monitor, which I don't usually do. It was the award-winning film *The Help,* which I kept hearing about but hadn't seen yet. The movie really got to me. The emotional story, coupled with my heightened emotional state along with some stuff that was going on in my life, caused me to sob so intensely that the guy sitting next to me leaned over, tapped me on the shoulder, and said, "Dude, are you all right?" Although I was momentarily confused and a bit embarrassed, since I had gotten so into the movie that I forgot I was sitting on a plane, I jumped right back into the film and let the tears continue to flow, which felt great and so cathartic.

As I look back at some of the most important, pivotal, and transformational moments of my life—both ones I considered to be good and ones I considered to be bad at the time—tears were a part of just about all of them.

How do you feel about shedding tears? Is it easy for you to cry? Is it hard? Are you comfortable crying in front of others? Do you judge yourself or others for doing so? I think it's interesting and important for us to ask ourselves these questions and notice our relationship to tears.

I'm not advocating that we go around crying all the time just for the sake of it. Excessive crying can sometimes point to a more serious underlying emotional issue or can be done as a way to manipulate others; I'm not talking about that, either. I'm talking about our ability to express our emotions in an authentic way, some of the time resulting in the shedding of tears. What if we embraced crying a bit more and let go of our negative connotations about doing so? As

Charles Dickens beautifully wrote in *Great Expectations*, "We need never be ashamed of our tears."

When we cry, we often open up, let down our guard, and connect with others in a more real and vulnerable way. Many times in my own life and with some of the clients I've worked with, I've seen tears dramatically shift a person's perspective, change the dynamic of an argument, and bring people together. Tears have a way of breaking down emotional walls and mental barriers we put up within ourselves and against others. Crying tends to be a human equalizer, because no matter the circumstance, situation, or stress we may face, our tears often have a way of shifting and altering things in a beautiful manner.

There's nothing wrong with our tears, even if we get a little embarrassed, uncomfortable, or pained when they show up. As we give ourselves permission to cry, we not only release toxins from our bodies, stress from our systems, and negative thoughts from our minds—we tap into one of the most basic and unifying experiences of being human. Crying is powerful and important. It's not only okay; it's essential.

CHAPTER 21

Swing Hard
(Just in Case You Hit It)

In July of 1992, the summer between my senior year in high school and my freshman year at Stanford, I got invited to play in the U.S. Junior National Baseball Championship tournament in Boise, Idaho. It was a pretty big deal. Some of the top high school players in the country were there, including a 16-year-old shortstop from Miami named Alex Rodriguez. So there we were, a group of pretty talented and confident (i.e., cocky) high school baseball players, but beneath the outward cockiness was a deep sense of insecurity, especially being around other players of this caliber.

The first day we were on the field, they sent us down to the batting cage. We were all standing around watching as each of us took turns hitting. Given the nature of the tournament, the group, and the fact that this was the first time we were on the field together, we were all definitely trying to impress one another. While we were all pretty good ballplayers and relatively impressive, there was one guy on our team, named Geoff Jenkins, who was literally like a man among boys when he stepped into the batting cage.

Geoff was an unbelievably talented player, and I'd played against him in summer ball the year before. He had this huge swing. Lots of coaches and scouts would comment on it, saying, "He won't be able to get away with that huge swing at the next level." Geoff was heading to play at University of Southern California that fall and since I was going to Stanford, we were going to be facing one another in the coming years at the college level.

As he was in the batting cage that day, he was putting on such an incredible display of hitting that, even in the midst of our cockiness and posturing, we were all looking around at each other in amazement at what he was doing. At one point, toward the end of his round of batting practice, Geoff swung so hard that on his backswing when he slammed the bat down, he actually cracked the wooden platform under his feet. I'd never seen anyone do that. He had to stop early and come out of the cage. The maintenance crew had to go in and try to figure out what they needed to do—either fix or remove the platform.

As Geoff walked out of the cage with his bat over his shoulder, knowing that he'd just been quite impressive, he had a sly, pleased-with-himself look on his face. One of the other guys on our team said, "Geoff, dude, why do you swing so hard?" Geoff stopped, spit, looked back at him, and, after a long pause, said, "Just in case I hit it."

I remember thinking, *Wow, that's not how I usually approach baseball, or life for that matter.*

Geoff went on to be an all-American while playing at USC and then a first-round draft pick of the Milwaukee Brewers. By the age of 23, he was a starter in the major leagues, where he played for 11 seasons—including winning a World Series ring with the Philadelphia Phillies in 2008, his final season. He never stopped swinging hard, and throughout his very successful major league career, he got quite a few hits (1,293 total) and hit a lot of home runs (221 total). He also struck out 1,186 times.

Far too often we hold back and play safe in life—worrying that we might fail, mess up, or embarrass ourselves. Some of this we do consciously, but much of it is unconscious; it's almost hardwired into us to do whatever we can to avoid looking bad.

A number of years ago, I was running in my neighborhood. In those days, when Samantha was still very young and before Rosie was even born, I used to get up before anyone was awake and go for a morning run. I was coming to my favorite part of the run (the end) and whenever I would get to the corner near our house, I would kick it into high gear, so I could "finish strong." That morning I was having a pretty good run and was really into the song on my iPod, so when I got to the corner, I took off even faster than normal. Sadly, I wasn't paying attention to the ground and didn't notice a big lip in the sidewalk. I hit it with my foot, and I went down—hard! I hadn't fallen down that hard in years. My iPod flew out of my hand, my hat came off my head, and I caught myself inches before hitting my chin on the pavement. As shocked as I was to have fallen, as I was lying there on the ground, before I stopped to assess my physical condition, I immediately looked up to see if anyone had seen what had happened. It was a reflex. Once I saw that there were no cars driving by and no one else on the street, I finally took a moment to think about my injuries. I was a little scraped up, although not that bad, and I had bumped my knee pretty good on the ground, but it didn't seem to be actually injured, just a little sore. I got up, brushed myself off, and, as I limped the rest of the way home, all I thought was, *Well, at least no one saw that.* It was a painful and humbling reminder of my own attachment to looking good (or, at the very least, not looking bad).

What if we weren't so concerned with messing up or looking bad? This is about being willing to take risks, be bold, and "swing hard" in our lives. And although this concept is pretty simple and we all understand it, like many things in life, understanding something is quite different from actually practicing it. In other words, it's much easier said than done.

Being bold, while scary and challenging at times, is essential to living an authentic and fulfilling life. Boldness is about stepping up and stepping out onto our "edge"— pushing the limits of what we think is possible for us. It's about living with courage and passion, and letting go of our attachment to the outcome along with the perceptions and opinions of others (including our gremlin). Living this way is not only thrilling, it's how we consciously evolve as human beings.

Will we swing and miss sometimes? Yes. Might we fall down and embarrass ourselves? Of course we will. But, as Wayne Gretzky famously said, "You miss 100 percent of the shots you never take."

CHAPTER 22

Embrace Powerlessness

A while back during one of our sessions, I was talking to my counselor Eleanor about the pain, embarrassment, and disappointment I continue to feel at times about my physical appearance and aging process—specifically my thinning hair. She said to me, "Mike, it sounds like embracing powerlessness is something that would benefit you right now." When she said this, a chill went down my spine and my body tightened up. "What do you mean, 'embrace powerlessness'?" I asked. "Why would I want to do that?"

Powerlessness seemed almost like a dirty word to me, at least to my ego, for sure. I pride myself on being a powerful person and I'm in the business of empowering others, so I couldn't imagine what embracing powerlessness even meant, let alone see the value in doing it. But, I gave Eleanor the benefit of the doubt and continued to listen. She went on to say, "Allowing yourself to *feel* powerless doesn't mean you *are* powerless. In fact, the more willing you are to embrace the *feeling* of powerlessness when it shows up, the more authentic power you'll be able to access." She then taught me a simple meditation/visualization technique to embrace the feeling of powerlessness, which I've been using for the past two years.[2] It's been incredibly liberating.

---

[2] Specific instructions for how to do this meditative technique yourself, as well as a link to the page on my website where you can download a free audio recording of me guiding you through it verbally, are listed in the appendix section of the book on page 203.

Through this process, I've realized that in many of the areas of my life where I've struggled most, one of the key factors has been my inability to acknowledge, feel, or embrace powerlessness. Instead, I often end up erroneously attempting to force outcomes in the name of being "responsible" or "powerful," when what is usually driving me is fear and the need to control (hence the struggle).

I saw my friend and fellow author/speaker Chip Conley speak at the Wisdom 2.0 business conference in San Francisco a while back. He opened his speech with the serenity prayer, which I appreciated and heard differently that day based on the work I'd been doing with Eleanor regarding powerlessness—"God, grant me the serenity to accept the things I cannot change; the courage to change the things I can; and the wisdom to know the difference." I've always had a bit of a reaction to this prayer and its underlying wisdom—not wanting to fully acknowledge the idea that there are actually things I *cannot* change. However, this prayer is all about consciously embracing our own powerlessness, and there's true brilliance in its simplicity and insight.

What if we stopped obsessing about the things we think need to be fixed about life, others, and ourselves—especially those things that are out of our control? What if we were able to bring a deeper level of acceptance and serenity to the difficulties in our lives, instead of piling loads of judgment, pressure, expectation, and more onto them (as well as ourselves and others)?

It's incredibly liberating when we're able to acknowledge, feel, and express our true emotions, even the ones we may not like, such as powerlessness. We tend to have lots of beliefs and a real hierarchy when it comes to emotions—deciding that some are good and others are bad. The reality is that emotions are positive when we feel and express them in a healthy way and negative when we suppress them. We've all had lots of positive experiences in life when we've had the courage to feel and express what we judge and consider "bad" emotions (e.g., fear, sadness, anger, jealousy, dread, hurt, shame, and so on). We've also had negative and painful experiences when we've withheld or suppressed what we consider "good" emotions (e.g., love, excitement, passion, gratitude, and so on).

The meditative technique that Eleanor taught me for embracing powerlessness also works with any other emotion we may be having difficulty feeling (usually the "bad" ones). However, remembering that just because we *feel* sad doesn't mean we *are* sad, or just because we *feel* jealous doesn't mean we *are* jealous, is an empowering distinction.

It's also important to remember that human emotions aren't sustainable. They are meant to be felt and expressed so they can then pass through us beautifully. This is why we often feel much better after a good cry. The more conscious we are about our emotions and the more willing we are to feel and express them—the happier, healthier, and more alive we become.

As I've allowed myself to embrace my own feelings of powerlessness (and other emotions that are challenging for me), even though it can be a bit scary and uncomfortable, especially at first, I've experienced a deeper level of peace and power in regard to some stressful circumstances in my life.

Embracing powerlessness can fundamentally shift our outlook on life and liberate us from a great deal of undue and unnecessary pressure, struggle, and expectation that we put on ourselves.

CHAPTER 23

Be Willing to Talk about Difficult Things

In July of 2010, Michelle and I found out, surprisingly, that we were expecting our third child. Since this wasn't something we'd planned, we were shocked, excited, and a bit freaked out, all at the same time, as we started to imagine our life with another baby. We began telling lots of people about this big news.

Within just a few days of learning about the pregnancy, however, we had a miscarriage—something we'd never been through and weren't at all prepared for. The emotions we experienced during that week, and in the weeks that followed, were quite intense. I felt sad, confused, and even relieved, although the feeling of relief was coupled with a deep feeling of shame, and some hardcore self-judgment and self-criticism. Michelle's experience, although similarly mixed emotionally, was different from mine, which just added to the complexity of it all.

As we moved through this painful experience, Michelle and I both got to a place of peace and gratitude—choosing to believe that this happened for a reason. While it was difficult, it turned out to be a very rich time of growth and connection for us.

One of the most complicated aspects of the whole experience was sharing it with others, which we were forced to do given that we had told a lot of people about the pregnancy as soon as we found out. Many people don't talk about their pregnancies until the second trimester, since the majority of miscarriages take place in those first three months. I understand, even more so now, why people keep this private—talking about a miscarriage can be quite emotional and uncomfortable for everyone involved.

However, even though it was an intense process for us and many of the people we talked to about it—especially those who had gone through this same experience—Michelle and I were so grateful for the amazing love and support we received. We were also blown away by how many other people had experienced a miscarriage—some we knew about, but many we didn't.

Even in the midst of this personal and emotional experience, I was fascinated by the human phenomenon of authenticity at play. There is such power available for us when we get real. And while I do believe that it's important for each of us to make conscious choices about what we share and with whom, far too often we choose not to share certain thoughts, feelings, or experiences because we deem them to be inappropriate or too much for people to handle. In other words, we don't allow ourselves to let people know what's really going on with us due to our fear of making them uncomfortable, of being judged, or of being disappointed by their response.

Sadly, in this process of withholding our true experiences and feelings, we miss out on opportunities to connect with people in an authentic way, get support, and share love, wisdom, and empathy. We also tend to focus so much on our own experience and our fears about what other people's perception of us might be that we forget that having conversations about difficult things can actually be liberating and healing for everyone involved. A number of people I talked with about our miscarriage thanked me, and, in some cases, when I talked to people who had been through this same experience, I both appreciated their wisdom and insight and could tell that talking about it with me was helpful and healing for them. I even chose to write a blog post about it and to share this experience with a larger group of people, which I was a little concerned about initially. The response to my blog post was overwhelmingly positive, and lots of people responded with their own stories, as well as with an overall statement that it's so important for us to talk about things like this, even if it's hard. When we do, we learn that we don't have to go through these things alone; there is a lot more support out there for us than we realize.

This is also true when the difficult experience is something that someone close to us is going through. Talking to them about it and supporting them can be tricky for different reasons—the nature of our relationship, their personality, or what type of support they want or need (which we may or may not know specifically). However, the biggest factor has to do with us—our awareness, empathy, and willingness to engage. While of course we want to respect their process, too often we make erroneous assumptions about what will best support them or we avoid engaging with them because we're not sure how to handle it (or because what they're going through is something we can't relate to).

When I was in seventh grade, my good friend Brian's dad died. I don't even know how old his dad was—but he wasn't an old man, he wasn't sick, he just had a heart attack and died one night. It was sad, scary, and confusing for me, especially at 13 years old, to think about someone's parent dying. While it wasn't the first time I'd experienced death, it was one of the first times a close friend of mine had lost a parent and it was hard for me to comprehend. I felt for Brian and his family, and couldn't imagine what he was going through. It also scared me as I thought about my own parents dying and what that would be like—although I did everything I could not to "go there," since at that age thinking of my mom or my dad dying was beyond terrifying.

Brian was out of school for a little while and when he came back, I didn't really know what to say to him. I felt uncomfortable being around him because I assumed he was upset and grieving the loss of his father. However, not knowing what that felt like and not wanting to say the wrong thing, I mostly avoided him. The few times we did talk, I tried to keep the conversation light and talk about relatively positive and superficial things so as not to upset him.

About a week or so after Brian came back to school, he pulled me aside to talk.

He said, "Mike, you haven't said anything about my dad or asked me how I'm doing since he died."

"Wow, Brian," I said. "I'm really sorry. I didn't know what to say."

He looked me square in the eyes and said, "Well, you could've just said that."

While this conversation was difficult and uncomfortable, and I walked away from it feeling guilty and embarrassed, I'm so grateful that Brian had the awareness and the courage to say that to me—quite an important life lesson in seventh grade. His humbling feedback taught me that it's more important to say something and to let people know we care, than it is to say the "right" thing. I'm grateful to have learned that at such a young age, although there are certain times and situations where I still have to remind myself about this.

Life can get messy and things happen that we're not sure how to handle. We aren't supposed to have it all figured out or know the "right" thing to say in every situation. The important thing to remember is that when we're willing to be real about the tough stuff that happens, we give ourselves the opportunity to learn, heal, grow, and connect—all things that are fundamentally important to the journey of life.

CHAPTER 24

Practice Gratitude

I had a simple but powerful conversation with a cabdriver a few years back that had a profound impact on me. I was in Houston, Texas, on my way back to the airport to fly home after speaking at a conference. The driver and I began talking. He had a beautiful accent. Based on how he looked and sounded, I assumed he was from somewhere in Africa, but I couldn't tell exactly where. It didn't come up in what we were talking about, so I didn't ask.

Right before we got to the airport, however, there was a pause in our conversation, so I inquired, "By the way, where are you from originally?"

"I'm from Ethiopia," he said. He then proudly stated, "I've been here in the U.S. for twenty years. I'm an American citizen now; so are both of my boys and my wife."

I'm not exactly sure what prompted me, but I then asked him, "What's your perspective on American culture, given that you didn't grow up here?"

At first he didn't say anything, and I thought maybe I had offended him. We were just arriving at the airport. He pulled up to the curb, put the cab in park, turned around, and looked me right in the eye.

"Can I be honest with you?" he asked.

"Sure," I said.

"Well," he said, "I think most people in this culture act like *spoiled brats*."

"Why do you say that?" I asked.

"Look, I'm from Ethiopia," he said. "Every day here is a good day."

I was taken aback by the simplicity, wisdom, and power of his statement. And, I was grateful for the reminder.

I've been speaking and writing about gratitude for many years, and I'm still amazed at how challenging it can be to focus on what I'm grateful for at times. We live in a culture that has an obsession with negativity, and it's easy for us to get caught up in how "bad" things are, as well as in our own personal and insatiable desire for more, thinking that what we have and how things are in our own lives are never quite good enough. However, regardless of the specific circumstances of our lives, even and especially when they're difficult, if we stop, pay attention, and look for it, there are always so many things we can be grateful for—if we choose to be. Gratitude is a practice, not a concept. And, like any other practice, the more genuine and consistent we are with it, the more valuable and beneficial it is.

Most of us, especially those of us on a path of personal growth and discovery, know that gratitude is important. We've heard about it, read about it, and been taught about it for years. In the mid-1990s, a wonderful book called *Simple Abundance* by Sarah Ban Breathnach came out. Sarah was a featured guest on *The Oprah Winfrey Show*, and Oprah talked about how Sarah's suggestion to keep a daily gratitude journal—to write down five things each day that you're grateful for—had a profound impact on her life. Oprah became a passionate advocate for the power of gratitude and since that time has continued to encourage millions of people around the world to keep their own gratitude journals.

Like so many other people, I took Oprah's advice and started my own journal many years ago. I found it to be fun, inspiring, and empowering to look for, find, and write down things I was grateful for. When I started speaking, coaching, and writing, much of my work focused on gratitude and appreciation. The technique of the gratitude journal was something I often suggested to people. However, over time it became one of the many things that I "know" and even "teach," but had stopped practicing consistently in my own life.

A few years back, as a New Year's resolution, I recommitted myself to the practice of my gratitude journal. I bought a new, beautiful journal and decided I was going to start using it. It took me a little while to get back into the practice of writing in it consistently, but once I was in the swing of it, it was pretty easy. Later that year I had a few months where things were going really well in many important areas of my life. As I sat down to write in my gratitude journal one morning, I decided to look back at some of the things I'd written over the past few months. As I turned the pages, I realized that I hadn't missed a day of writing in over three months. I was amazed. It was less about the consistency of my writing, and more about the consistency of my excitement to do this exercise and the benefits I got from it. Things were going so well in my life, and the positive turns seemed to be directly connected to my use of the gratitude journal. I said to Michelle, "I'm not sure if things are going so well because I'm writing in my gratitude journal every day, or I'm excited to write in my gratitude journal every day because things are going so well. I bet it's a combination of both. At some level, I don't really care—I'm just grateful for how things are going and for my journaling practice."

The way gratitude works is that the more we focus on feeling grateful, the more we have to feel grateful for. And while many of us have experienced this personally, recent scientific studies have concluded that gratitude can have significantly positive effects on our health, our moods, our productivity, and our relationships.

In one specific study, conducted by Robert A. Emmons, Ph.D., at the University of California at Davis and Mike McCullough at the University of Miami, participants were given one of three tasks. Each week, they kept a short journal. One group was asked to write down five things they were grateful for that had occurred in the past week, another was asked to record five hassles from the previous week that displeased them, and the neutral group was asked to list five events or circumstances that affected them, but they weren't told whether to focus on something positive or negative specifically.

Ten weeks later, the people in the gratitude group felt better about their lives as a whole, plus they reported fewer health complaints, and they exercised more.

Like many other things in life that we know are good for us (exercise, eating healthy, sleeping enough, drinking lots of water, telling the truth, and so on), it's not the knowledge that will benefit us; it's the practice. The amazing thing about gratitude is that there's no "right" way to practice being grateful. Whether you choose to keep a journal, thank the people around you, use positive affirmations, ask other people what they're grateful for (one of my favorites), focus on gratitude in your quiet time of prayer or meditation, or simply remind yourself to slow down and breathe—taking time to focus on what we're grateful for is one of the easiest and most effective ways to empower ourselves, calm ourselves down, and remember what matters most in life.

As one of my mentors said to me years ago, "Gratitude and victimhood can't coexist."

CHAPTER 25

Have the Courage to Be Vulnerable

Given the focus of my work, especially in the past five years since the release of my book *Be Yourself, Everyone Else Is Already Taken*, which is all about authenticity and vulnerability, I'm constantly in situations where I'm talking about, encouraging, and seeing the positive impact of vulnerability.

Because of my baseball background, I'm sometimes invited to speak to athletes, specifically baseball players. A few years ago, I got invited down to spring training to speak to a group of minor league players for one of the Major League Baseball organizations. This was a big deal for me and I was excited to have an opportunity to speak to these guys, given that I had stood in their shoes in my early 20s. I could relate specifically to what they were going through—spring training is an exciting but stressful time, where lots of evaluation takes place and decisions are made. A number of those guys would be released (i.e., cut) by the end of spring training, so how they performed over the next few weeks would have a big impact on not only their season but also their future baseball careers (or lack thereof).

I spoke to them that morning about how they could effectively deal with the pressure of spring training and how they could handle the mental and emotional ups and downs of playing baseball in a healthy and productive way. My talk went well and seemed to resonate with the guys. After I spoke, a number of them came up to talk to me. In addition to their comments and questions about my speech, a bunch of them wanted to tell me about something that happened a few days earlier. Because I heard about it passionately from a number of different guys (and got a few different versions of the same story), I wanted to find out more about what went down, so I asked my friend and former Stanford teammate AJ, who was running the whole minor league system for this organization at the time, what had happened.

AJ told me that he had asked his coaches to introduce themselves to the players at their first all-camp meeting the week before in a unique way. Instead of them giving their résumés, he wanted each of them to tell a personal story about a meaningful moment they'd had when they were players themselves. He said it was amazing and that one of his coaches, named Alan, blew everyone away with his story.

Alan got up and said, "I played for ten years in Triple-A's, without a single day in the major leagues."

No one plays in AAA (which is the highest level of the minor leagues) for ten years. If you get that high up and hang around for a while, you either make it up to the big leagues, or you walk away from the game. It's very uncommon and actually quite difficult to spend that much time at that level of the minors. Alan went on to say:

> I played for a number of different organizations, but couldn't break through and make it. Toward the end of that tenth season in Triple-A's, I finally made peace with the fact that I wasn't going to make it. I was disappointed, of course, but because

I'd given it everything I had, and it just didn't seem like it was meant to be, I was actually okay with it.

Once I made my decision, I called my dad because we'd been talking about my career in the recent weeks. I said to him, "Dad, I've decided I'm going to retire. I'm not going to quit right now because the season's not over, but when it ends, I'm going to stop playing. Would you do me a favor, Dad? Can you come see me play one last time? That would really mean a lot to me."

When my dad got there, I was fired up. I really wanted to play well. He was going to be in town for five nights. The first night he was in town, I came up to bat in the second inning, hit a ground ball to second base, and grounded out. When I got back in the dugout, my manager walked over to me, tapped me on the shoulder, and told me to sit down.

He took me out of the game, and in the second inning. Now that only happens if you don't hustle, do something stupid, or get hurt. But I wasn't hurt, I did hustle on that play—I always hustled—and I hadn't done anything stupid to warrant him taking me out of the game that early.

I didn't understand. And I was mad. I didn't say anything to my manager because I didn't want to be disrespectful. But, how could he show me up like that, and in front of my father? Anyway, I just sat there at the end of the bench about as far away from the manager as I could.

Then, I heard someone at the other end of the bench say, "Can we tell him?" The next thing I knew, my manager walked all the way down to the end of the bench and got right in my face.

He said, "Do you want to know why I took you out of the game?"

"Yes sir," I said. "I didn't appreciate that; you showed me up in front of my father."

"Well," my manager said, "I took you out of the game because you just got called up to the major leagues."

The next thing I knew, I looked up and all twenty-five guys on my team had gathered around me in the dugout to give me hugs and high fives. Those guys were so excited for me because they all knew how long I'd waited, how hard I'd worked, and how much it meant to me. The celebration went on so long in the dugout, they actually had to stop the game.

As amazing as this story is, the most incredible part is that when this coach told this story to a roomful of 150 Minor League Baseball players, he broke down and cried in front of all of them. That never happens there, *ever*. And a few days later, dozens of those players were coming up to talk to me about it because it had a huge impact on them.

That's how powerful it is when we have the courage to be vulnerable—when we let people see who we really are and how we really feel.

Dr. Brené Brown, author of *Daring Greatly*, is a psychologist and research professor from the University of Houston who studies human emotions, including shame and vulnerability. In a March 2012 TED talk, she said, "Vulnerability is not weakness, and that myth is profoundly dangerous." She went on to say that after 12 years of research, she has actually determined that vulnerability is "our most accurate measurement of courage."

Unfortunately, all too often we relate to vulnerability—especially in certain environments, relationships, and situations—as something we should avoid at all costs. However, it's vulnerability that liberates us from our erroneous and insatiable obsession with trying to do everything "right"—thinking we can't make mistakes, have flaws, or be human. In other words, being vulnerable allows us to let go of the pressure-filled, stress-inducing perfection demands we place on ourselves.

In addition to our own liberation, when we're vulnerable we give other people permission to be vulnerable as well, and in so doing, we open up the possibility of real human connection and the opportunity to impact people in a profound way, which is what most of us truly want in life.

CHAPTER 26

Trust Yourself

By the summer of 2004, my relationship with Michelle had come to a crossroads. We'd been together for almost four years and had been living together for more than two. The main point of contention in our relationship had to do with our future (i.e., when and if we were going to get married). Michelle was just about to turn 34 and I was 31.

We talked about our future quite a bit—she really wanted to get married and start a family. While I, too, wanted those things, I didn't feel that I was ready yet. During our conversations, we both did a pretty good job of listening to one another and being as compassionate as possible, but, in our lower moments, it would get sticky, painful, and sometimes even ugly. Michelle would start to push and I would start to pull away—a classic, stereotypical male/female dynamic in relationships, particularly related to commitment.

I knew that if I chose to marry Michelle because I felt pressured by her or our friends, or even because "it was time," we'd been together long enough, and we were at the right age, I'd resent myself or her, and it wouldn't work. And, while I was aware of some of my own fears and doubts about the idea of getting married—to Michelle and in general—I hadn't really looked at or owned some of the deeper issues that were getting in my way.

In the middle of that summer, she and I went down to San Diego to participate in a three-day workshop called "The Shadow Process," delivered by the late author and teacher Debbie Ford. We were both big fans of Debbie's work and had heard great things about this program. The Shadow Process is all about coming face-to-face with our "shadow"—all the parts of ourselves that we've tried to hide or deny, the parts we believe are not acceptable to our family, friends, and, most important, us. Our shadow is also made up of everything that annoys, horrifies, or disgusts us about other people or about ourselves. In the workshop, we were given the opportunity to both confront and make peace with various aspects of our "dark" side, as a way to liberate us from our fear, judgment, and denial.

I loved it! It was intense, of course, but absolutely transformational. Given what was going on between Michelle and me, I related everything I was learning and experiencing in the workshop to our relationship. Initially, I found myself focusing on all the reasons why I thought we shouldn't get married—and why it seemed like I couldn't fully trust Michelle. I had had trust issues for much of my life—growing up with a single mom, without a lot of money, and in Oakland had forced me to become "street smart" and to have to rely on myself in many ways. In my case, this involved not trusting people easily. I spent a lot of time and energy waiting for people to disappoint me, let me down, and leave. I prided myself on not being needy or dependent, which was how I often justified not being intimate or vulnerable.

As I started to look more deeply, beyond some of the drama from my past, and get more in touch with how I was actually feeling, I realized that my trust issues had nothing to do with Michelle. What I realized for the very first time in my life was that I didn't trust *myself*.

I was terrified to get married and was worried that if we did I would ruin our relationship, her life, and the lives of the kids we might have. I thought, *What if I fail, cheat on her, hurt her, hurt our kids, get depressed again, lose interest, don't have what it takes, end up being a total loser as a husband and father, or die?* All of these things seemed horrible, which is why I'd been denying them. I realized I was avoiding them unconsciously or hoping they would just go away so I would be "ready" to get married.

Realizing this was quite painful and humbling at first— but ultimately it was liberating. I knew that running from these fears or pretending they didn't exist wouldn't work. I needed to own them if I was ultimately going to trans- form them. As vulnerable and scared as I felt to admit these things, I sat down with Michelle and shared them all with her. She wasn't upset; in fact, she was grateful I was willing to be so open. We had a series of wonderfully authentic and heartfelt conversations that weekend about our relation- ship, the future, and the fears that we both felt.

The most important moment of the workshop for me happened on the final day. I asked myself a simple but im- portant question: *If I trusted myself fully, what would I do?* The answer was clear and obvious—I would ask Michelle to marry me. Three weeks later, I proposed. She said yes and the following summer we got married!

Trusting ourselves doesn't mean that we won't get scared, have doubts, or make mistakes—all of which are in- evitable in life. Trust is a choice we make in the moment. It is choosing to empower our belief in ourselves over our fears of what might go wrong. It's not about avoiding or denying our fears, it's about having faith in something that is bigger and more powerful than fear: us.

It's understandable that many of us struggle to trust ourselves, especially at certain times, in certain situations, and with certain people. We tend to remember the times we've failed, made mistakes, or done things that in hindsight we judge as unworthy of trust. However, self-trust is, like most things in life, a present-moment phenomenon. As soon as we reach back into the past to determine if we're worthy of trust or capable of trusting ourselves, we give away our power.

Self-trust is a lifelong journey and something we continue to grow into as we evolve. For some of us, it's easier than for others. It's important for us to be mindful and compassionate with ourselves in regard to self-trust. I'm grateful to see my own capacity for self-trust continue to expand, especially in the past few years. And, I'm also aware that there are times that it's extremely challenging for me to trust myself. Eleanor said something to me in a session we had a while back that resonated with me about this. She said, "Mike, you actually do trust yourself quite a bit, you just don't think it's safe to trust yourself, so you end up second-guessing yourself a lot."

However easy or difficult it is for you to trust yourself, remember that listening to your inner wisdom, trusting your own instincts, and relying on yourself in a healthy way to make decisions in your life are the best things you can do to liberate yourself from unnecessary fear and stress, and to empower yourself in every aspect of your life.

CHAPTER 27

Remember that You Are Much More than What You Do

In June of 1993, I woke up in the Stanford hospital in a daze. In addition to being out of it, I was in an enormous amount of pain and unclear what had happened and why I was there. Over the course of the next 24 hours, as I re-qained consciousness and some of the medication they'd given to me began to wear off, I learned that in the middle of the night I'd had a freak accident.

It was finals week of my freshman year at Stanford and my friends and I wanted to blow off a little steam, so we threw a party in our dorm room. I ended up drinking a lot, which was something I was doing quite a bit in those days, and had a vague recollection of our night of partying. At some point after midnight, I passed out in my bed, which was the top bunk of one of the two bunk beds in our two-room dorm. My bed, which we had moved a few months earlier, was pushed up against the wall right next to a set of big windows. At some point not that long after I fell asleep, I rolled out of my bed, and out of the window, and fell two stories down to the concrete terrace 15 to 20 feet below. To make matters worse, or at least more embarrassing, I was completely naked at the time.

In hindsight, it was probably a blessing that I was as drunk as I was and had passed out because, amazingly, I fell in such a way that I did a relatively small amount of damage in what otherwise could have been a catastrophic accident. I broke my wrist, I broke my pelvis, and I had slight compression fractures on two of my lumbar vertebrae. I also managed to scrape the side of my face on the back of the tire of a bicycle that was in the bike rack right next to where I fell.

Needless to say, when the reality of what had happened became clear to me and I realized what I'd done, I was filled with a deep sense of shame, embarrassment, and fear. In those first few days in the hospital, as they were assessing the extent of my injuries, we weren't sure what was going to be required. Initially, the doctors thought they would need to operate on my back and fuse my bones together, which would've essentially ended my baseball career and impacted my physical mobility for the rest of my life. Once the swelling went down, thankfully, they realized they would not need to do such an extensive procedure. It turned out that with a back brace, a cast on my arm, lots of rest and recovery time over the summer, and some good fortune, I was going to be just fine and might even be able to continue playing baseball in the fall.

My freshman year at Stanford had been a difficult one for me. While I was excited to be in college and enjoying the Stanford experience for the most part, a different injury to my pitching arm had forced me to miss the entire baseball season, have a minor elbow surgery, and put my baseball future in jeopardy. Since much of my identity was tied up in my being a baseball player, it had been very difficult to spend the entire season not playing. I stayed at home when the team went on the road. I watched the games from the dugout when the team played at home. I'd never been injured before like this and I felt like a loser. The thing that made me feel special and important in life was being a good baseball player. During my freshman year, not playing left me feeling lost, and the fear of not being able to play in the future left me feeling terrified. I'm sure my bouts of excessive drinking that year were directly related to my feelings of self-loathing, my lack of identity, and my fear of the future.

As painful as that week in the hospital was, there were two incredible and enlightening aspects of it. First of all, as each day passed, the news about my injuries and my prognosis got better. By the time I left, it seemed pretty clear to me that, while I'd probably be in a lot of pain over the summer and I had to take things easy, I was going to be just fine. I felt incredibly grateful and blessed because it was made abundantly clear to me by many of the doctors that I was lucky to be alive and still able to walk. I had come close to losing my life or having it changed dramatically, and this reality had put a lot of things into perspective. Although I was deeply shaken by this experience, I also felt incredibly fortunate.

Second of all, the response from my friends and fellow classmates was incredible. They came to visit me in the hospital. They brought notes, cards, flowers, and balloons. They told me how they felt about me and how important I was to them. I was touched deeply by the outpouring of support and appreciation. It helped as I was dealing with the pain of the accident, and the embarrassment I felt about all of it. What specifically amazed me was that there were all these people who I'd only known for that one year who seemed to really care about me and think I was a great guy.

But, they hadn't even seen me play baseball and that didn't seem to have anything to do with how they felt about me. This blew my mind. Because, at 19 years old, I thought what made me special was the fact that I was such a good athlete, but these people seemed to like me anyway.

I learned a great deal about myself, about life, and about what truly matters through that scary experience. Thankfully, I recovered fully from the accident and was able to resume my normal activities by the end of that summer, even being able to play baseball again when I returned to Stanford in the fall. But, the lessons of that experience have stayed with me, and I'm grateful for that.

Unfortunately, we often attach much of our value to what we do. And while there's nothing wrong with enjoying our work and being excited about what we do, it's important for us to remember that we are *much* more than that. As I travel around the world speaking to groups within a variety of different organizations, I meet lots of incredible, intelligent, and successful people—many of whom are passionate about the work they do. I also have had a chance to coach and speak to lots of entrepreneurs and people, like me, who have their own businesses in which they are committed to empowering and supporting others. Many of these folks eat, breathe, and sleep their work—which is both inspiring and at times a little scary.

When we define ourselves by our work and what we do, we end up putting an enormous amount of pressure on ourselves—living and dying by the results we produce, our reputation, or a variety of external circumstances and situations, much of which we can't control.

In her book *The Top Five Regrets of the Dying*, Bronnie Ware, who worked for a number of years directly with people who were dying, says one of the main regrets people have at the end of their lives is, "I wish I hadn't worked so hard."

A few weeks ago, as I was writing this book, I saw a Facebook post from a friend of mine about a friend of his from high school who had died suddenly in an accident. He was just about my age, and as I looked at the posts on his Facebook page, although I didn't know him, I could feel the sadness, love, shock, and gratitude being expressed about him, his life, and his death. As I scrolled through the many photos, posts, and expressions of condolences, I was struck by what a vibrant spirit this man had and moved by all of the photos of parties, gatherings, adventures, and good times. After spending quite a bit of time looking at all of this, I was struck by the fact that I couldn't tell what he did for a living and no one even mentioned it in any of the posts. Maybe his career wasn't all that important to him or he hadn't had much professional "success" in his life. Regardless of the circumstances, reading these heartfelt posts and thinking about the sudden death of someone so close to my own age made me stop and think more deeply about who I am and what matters.

In many ways, when it's all said and done, what we do is way less important than who we are. And, when we can remember that, it gives us a healthy and important perspective about how to live life, engage in our work, and focus on what's most important.

CHAPTER 28

Roll with Life

In March of 2013, I got an offer from Hay House, whom I'd been hoping to work with for some time, to publish the book that you're reading right now. I was elated, humbled, and grateful. For the first time in a number of years, I actually felt ready and excited to write a new book.

For the past few years, when people would ask me what my next book was going to be about, I would often say, "I have a few different ideas, but am not one hundred percent sure yet. I do know one thing, for sure, about my next book—it's going to be an enjoyable experience to write." Putting together each of my first two books was quite stressful for me, for different reasons.

When I wrote *Focus on the Good Stuff*, I had a lot of insecurity and fear of the unknown, since it was my first time. In addition, we had a new baby at home, so trying to figure out how to write a book, run my business, and be there for Michelle and Samantha all at the same time posed lots of challenges.

With *Be Yourself, Everyone Else Is Already Taken*, although I had written a book before, I had more demands and expectations on my time, and we also had a two-year-old at home and another baby on the way. A busy daddy, pregnant mommy, and passionate toddler don't often combine to make the most peaceful home environment. On top of this, the manuscript and the new baby were both due right around the same time, so the pressure was on.

For this third book, I decided I was going to create a stress-free, drama-free writing experience. My plan was to get started a little bit in the spring—gather notes and ideas, and start putting the outline of the book together. But, given the nature of my speaking and travel schedule, I planned to focus most of my attention on writing during the summer. Specifically, I planned to take the month of July off and not schedule any speaking engagements, meetings, or anything else—so that I could fully focus on the book. One of the things I've learned about myself in the past is that if I immerse myself in the process, I can actually write quite a bit in a relatively short amount of time. On the flip side, it's very difficult for me to write just a little bit every day in the midst of my daily life.

Because of the nature of my business, although I try to take time off when I can, I usually don't take a full month off from speaking engagements, events, and marketing activities in the middle of the year. The only other time I've done this in the past has been in December, when things are often pretty quiet business-wise during the holiday season. Taking the whole month of July off felt a little scary, but mostly exciting, given that I was looking forward to having some dedicated time to just focus on the book. I hadn't gotten as much done leading up to July as I had planned, but I was hopeful that the month off would be productive.

However, on June 26th, we got an e-mail from the owner of the house we'd been renting for the previous two years letting us know that he was putting it on the market and he wanted us to move out. We had spoken to him about the lease the month before, and the plan had been for us to re-sign for another year at the end of July, so this was a big change in plans. All of a sudden, we had to find a new house. And, the month of July that I was planning to use primarily for writing was now going to involve finding a new house, packing, and moving—yikes!

Needless to say, this threw Michelle and me for a bit of a loop. After a couple days of panic, we picked ourselves up off the floor and began to look for a new house. Amazingly, within about a week, we found a great new house on an incredible street (at the end of a cul-de-sac with lots of kids the girls' same age). We got the house and were elated, although now there was the issue of packing up our entire house and my office, and moving everything in a relatively short amount of time in the midst of trying to get some work done on the book so that I could actually attempt to finish it on time. The manuscript was due on August 31st— so much for the drama-free, stress-free writing experience I was planning.

While there were definitely some interesting twists, turns, and bumps in the road, and I wouldn't categorize it as "smooth sailing" by any stretch, amazingly everything got done on time, without too much trouble. What allowed for this to happen were a few specific things. First of all, we got some great support from a number of people around us. Second of all, amazing and heroic work was done by Michelle in taking care of so many aspects of the house, the girls, and our lives. And third, and probably most important, was *surrendering* to the experience as it was happening. There were times in the midst of the move and the writing process when I found myself resisting what was going on. In those moments, things were very difficult, and I suffered. However, when I began allowing things to be exactly as they were—accepting and appreciating the reality of what was going on—all there really was to do was the next thing, which was whatever was right in front of me (packing or unloading a box, writing a chapter, and so on). And while it did take a lot of support, quite a bit of focus, and a few miracles along the way, it was a great reminder of the importance of rolling with life as it shows up.

All too often, we get overwhelmed by the enormity of a task or thinking that we have to do it all at once—instead of step by step, which is how everything gets done in life. Whether it's cleaning out our garage, organizing our desk, catching up on our e-mail, or working on a big project at work or at home, when we surrender to what's actually happening (and stop fighting against it), reach out for some support, and attempt to accomplish what's right in front of us, little by little, most things we have to deal with, even really big stuff, can be handled with a relative amount of ease. It's really up to us and how we relate to what's going on.

One of my absolute favorite quotes is from Byron Katie. She says, "When you argue with reality you lose, but only one hundred percent of the time."

CHAPTER 29

Speak Your Truth (Even if Your Voice Shakes)

Before Michelle and I got married, each of us wanted to put together a gathering with the respective important men and women in our lives to celebrate the end of our singlehood. These weren't bachelor or bachelorette parties in the standard sense; rather, we were looking to prepare for our wedding in a sacred way. We wanted to honor our single lives by authentically acknowledging all they had provided to us.

We each set up a time to go away on the same weekend with our respective groups of close friends about a month before our wedding ceremony. I gathered with a group of a dozen male friends at the home of one of the men who had a great place right on the water. We were excited to spend the weekend there, and looked forward to hanging out, going waterskiing, and catching up.

In addition to having fun and playing around on my friend's boat, I wanted to spend a few hours sitting in a circle with these men who were important in my life and talking through some of my thoughts and feelings related to getting married. One of the things that I'd brought with me was a folder of photos of the five other women in my life who I'd been in love with prior to meeting Michelle. I wanted to talk about each of them, as a way to honor them and acknowledge what I'd learned from them about life, love, and myself. Each of these women and my relationships with them had taught me a great deal and helped put me in the position I was in, feeling ready and excited to get married (albeit nervous as well). All five of these women had been important to me, and still were, even though our relationships had changed. I wanted to somehow include them in the experience, while at the same time release them as parts of my past.

Although I wanted to do this, I felt pretty weird about the possibility of actually talking to these men about my past loves. Even though I trusted the men in that circle very much, it felt potentially awkward and disrespectful for me to have a conversation about other women, especially right as I was preparing to marry Michelle. In addition, Michelle's brother Steve, my soon-to-be brother-in-law, was one of the men who would be sitting in that circle. I didn't know how that would feel for him or for me.

I brought the photos, put them in my bag, and thought that if it felt right and I had the courage to do so, I'd bring them out and talk about them. If not, they could just stay in my bag and no one would know. As we gathered and began to talk about various things, I was able to share vulnerably about some of my deepest thoughts and feelings related to getting married—my hopes, fears, dreams, worries, visions, and more. It was beautiful. I felt seen, honored, and blessed by my friends.

Given how safe I felt, I decided to reach into my bag and take out the photos. I said, "Michelle and I went to a wedding a few years ago—the friends of ours getting married had both been married previously. During the ceremony, they each acknowledged their ex-spouses and thanked them for all they had learned from them. I found it both odd and inspiring at the same time. In that vein, I brought with me photos of five different women, each of whom I was in love with at some point in my life before I met Michelle. These women were, and still are, important to me. I want to pass around each of the photos and tell you a little about them and what I learned from them."

I could tell by the looks on the faces around the circle that most of the men were both intrigued and a little caught off guard by this conversation. And while it did feel a bit weird, especially at first, and I could feel my heart racing and my voice shaking, as I got into it, it actually felt really good and empowering. The conversation didn't go on for all that long as I passed the photos around and talked about each of the women. However, once I finished, something amazing happened. One of my friends said, "Wow, Mike, thanks for having the courage to share these photos and your feelings about these women. I think about some of the women I've been in love with in the past from time to time, but I never talk about them out loud."

We proceeded as a group to have a remarkable conversation that lasted for a few hours, in which most of the men in that circle talked about some of their past relationships, particularly the ones that had been the most heartbreaking. It was one of the most intimate and beautiful conversations I've ever had with a group of men in my life. There were tears, there was laughter, and there was a profound sense of freedom and liberation from the openness and truth of that conversation.

I'm so glad I was willing to have that conversation with those men that day. Not only did it serve and support me as I was preparing to get married, it turned out to have a positive impact on everyone in that circle, which was be-yond my wildest expectations.

This is often what happens when we speak our truth—it enllveris us and has the possibility to inspire others. How-ever, it's important to remember that speaking our truth involves courage, awareness, and nonattachment.

Courage is about speaking up, even if we're scared. Sometimes our voice will shake, our knees will knock, and our heart will pound, but if we're willing to speak from our heart, our truth can both set us free and connect us with others in an authentic way.

Awareness is essential because we often confuse our *truth* with our *opinion,* and they are not the same thing. If you're anything like me, you probably have lots of opin-ions. There's nothing wrong with having and expressing opinions. However, many of our opinions are filled with righteous judgment and an arrogant sense that we're right and those who don't agree with us are wrong. Our truth runs much deeper than any of our opinions. Truth is about how we feel and what's real for us. Truth is not about being right; it's about expressing what we think and feel in a vul-nerable way.

For example, let's say I have a conflict with someone in my life because they sent me an e-mail that I thought was rude and disrespectful. If I were to talk to them (or even worse, e-mail them back) and say, "Your e-mail was rude and disrespectful," while that may be my honest opinion, it wouldn't be my deepest truth and most likely wouldn't lead to a resolution of the conflict. If I were to say to them, "Your e-mail upset me and hurt my feelings," that would express more of my truth. Our truth is about our emotional experi-ence. Our opinion is about our mental assessment.

And, if we can remember to let go of our attachment, speaking our truth becomes much easier. We often get attached to how people will perceive us. The reality is that we can't control other people's reactions to us or to anything we do or say. If we speak our truth with love, awareness, and authenticity, it will often be received well, even if those who hear it don't agree with what we're saying or feel the same way. However, sometimes it will upset, confuse, offend, or hurt others—even if that wasn't our intention. While we want to be as mindful and empathetic toward others as we can, speaking our truth is about being true to who we are and how we feel. And, as a popular saying goes, "Be who you are and say what you feel because those who mind don't matter and those who matter don't mind."

CHAPTER 30

Don't Sweat the Small Stuff

In March of 1998 I read a book that changed the trajectory of my life. That book was *Don't Sweat the Small Stuff*, by Richard Carlson. I received it in the mail just a few days before heading out to Florida for spring training with the Kansas City Royals. I'd injured my pitching arm the season before and had reconstructive elbow surgery. Although I was only 8 months into a 12- to 18-month rehab process and was doing everything I could to recover from the injury, I had a sense that my baseball career was probably over. With this as the backdrop, I had a lot on my mind as I made my way out to spring training that year. The power and simplicity of the message in Richard's book and the insight and perspective I gained while reading it were profound and very helpful. While my arm injury and the potential end of my baseball career didn't seem anything like "small stuff" to me, I realized in reading the book how easily I allowed little things to stress me out and cause pain and worry for me unnecessarily.

When I arrived in Florida, having read the book on the way out, I did something I'd never done before—I went and purchased five copies and sent them to my mom, my dad, my two sisters, and a good friend back home. I really wanted to share the inspiration and insight I'd gained from the book with some of the most important people in my life.

A few weeks into my time at spring training, I was notified by the Royals that they were releasing me from my contract, which meant I had to go home. They didn't think I was going to fully recover from my injury and be able to play, so they had decided to let me go. I was shocked and scared, although at some deep level, not completely surprised. While it wasn't officially the end of my career, it was a major blow, and it left me reeling. I packed up my stuff and began the long drive back to California just a few weeks after I'd made the long drive to Florida.

On my way home, I had a lot of time to contemplate my baseball career, my current situation, and my future. I was filled with a myriad of thoughts and feelings, many of which were conflicting. I felt scared and sad about the potential end of my career. I felt confused and worried about what this all meant and what would happen next. I also felt a sense of excitement and curiosity about what else I might be able to focus on and do with my life if, in fact, baseball would no longer be a part of it. In addition to all of these thoughts and feelings, I kept thinking about *Don't Sweat the Small Stuff* and Richard. On top of being inspired by the wisdom of his book, I was also inspired by his work. And although it wasn't the first time I'd had this thought, I realized that there was a part of me that wanted to do what Richard Carlson did—inspire others. I wasn't sure how one went about becoming an author like Richard, but I knew that he lived in the San Francisco Bay Area, not far from where I lived, and I wondered if I might be able to get in touch with him when I got home.

Although it was way out of my comfort zone (I'd never done anything like this before in my life), when I got home, I sent a letter to Richard thanking him for his beautiful book and inspiration. I also let him know about my current situation and the thoughts and desires I had about someday potentially doing the kind of work that he did. Given how busy and successful Richard was, I didn't really expect to hear back from him, but it felt important for me to write and send the letter anyway.

Amazingly, a few weeks later I received a three-page personal response from Richard in the mail. He thanked me for my heartfelt letter and shared some words of wisdom with me about my dream of becoming an author and teacher. "My suggestion to you if you want to get into this field is twofold. First of all, *be yourself*. Don't try to imitate anyone and their style, including mine. Second, find something that really touches you, not something you think is going to be popular, but something that is really you."

I was blown away that he'd taken the time to respond to me personally. I appreciated the truth and sincerity of his feedback. And, I took it as a sign that, like him, doing work that was intended to inspire others was something I was supposed to do.

Five years later, in the spring of 2003, Michelle and I attended a fund-raiser for a nonprofit organization called Challenge Day that we both love and support. I'd started my speaking and coaching business two years earlier in 2001, and I'd also begun working on my first book, but it was pretty slow going at that point. Richard and his wife, Kris, were both at this fund-raiser—I saw their names in the program. I leaned over to Michelle and said, "Oh my God, Richard Carlson is here!" We were sitting with our friends Rich and Kathy, and I knew that Rich knew Richard personally. When the event ended, I turned to Rich and said, "Hey, would you mind introducing me to Richard Carlson?"

He said, "I thought you guys already knew each other."

I said, "Well, I'm a huge fan of his work and we corresponded a few years ago, but we've never actually met."

We made our way up front, through the hundreds of people at the event, to where Richard was chatting with some friends. Rich introduced us, and I said, "Richard, it's such an honor to meet you! Thank you for your incredible work—your books have had a big impact on me. I doubt you remember, but I wrote you a letter about five years ago just as my baseball career was coming to an end. I was trying to figure out my next step in life. You were kind enough to write back, which I really appreciated."

Richard said, "I remember you and your letter. It's nice to finally meet you in person, Mike!"

We talked for a while. I told Richard a little bit about me and my current work as a speaker and coach. I also told him I had an idea for a book on the power of appreciation. Richard said, "The world could use a book on appreciation—it's such an important topic! Here's my card; feel free to get in touch with me if I can be of any help with your book."

I got in touch with Richard after meeting him at the event and we set up a time to meet for tea near his office. I was nervous and excited to connect with him one-on-one and wasn't quite sure what the conversation would involve. We ended up sitting and talking for almost three hours—about life, sports, family, appreciation, keeping things in perspective, writing and publishing, and many other things. It felt as though we'd known each other for a very long time. And, without me even asking, Richard offered to write the foreword for my book if I wanted him to (which, of course, I did), and he said he wanted to help me in whatever other way he could.

I was, once again, blown away and deeply grateful for his care, generosity, and offer of support. Over the next four years, Richard and I built a beautiful and wonderful relationship. He became my mentor, and being around him felt like being around the older brother I never had.

Sadly and unexpectedly, on December 13, 2006, just three weeks after he'd written the foreword for *Focus on the Good Stuff,* Richard died at the age of 45. He was flying to New York for a television appearance and he had a pulmonary embolism, a blood clot that moved into his lungs, from which he never woke up.

I learned so much from Richard through his work, our friendship, and watching how he lived his life and balanced his many responsibilities. He really walked his talk and had a presence about him that was remarkable. When you were with Richard, it felt like he didn't have anywhere else to be and that you were the most important person on the planet.

I miss him very much to this day, but I feel his presence with me all the time. As I was writing this book, which in many ways was directly inspired by Richard and the way he wrote his books, I would often hear his voice in my head, especially as I started to worry or stress out about something specific, saying, "Mike, remember, don't sweat it; it's not that big of a deal."

Richard's simple but profound message—that life's *not* an emergency; that most of what we get ourselves upset about is really small stuff; and that when we stop and take inventory, we have lots to be grateful for—is so true. Not sweating the small stuff is about keeping things in a healthy perspective and focusing on what truly matters in life. And when you remember this, as Richard said, "you will begin to create a more peaceful and loving you." He's right and I'm so grateful for the wisdom he shared with me and with all of us.

CHAPTER 31

Be Easily Amazed

Samantha was born on February 11, 2006. Her birth was one of the most amazing experiences of my life (in the truest sense of the word *amazing*). Of course, her being our first child, it was also pretty overwhelming on many levels. Although Samantha was born three and a half weeks early and Michelle's labor was incredibly intense (and without drugs), the birth was so remarkable and miraculous that it blew me away. At the moment she came out, I had a flood of emotion—joy, excitement, relief, gratitude, fear, and curiosity—and an overwhelming feeling of love. As the midwife caught her and we saw that she was healthy, the tears flowed.

In the midst of all the excitement, I had a funny feeling that this all seemed somewhat familiar to me. This feeling didn't make any rational sense, since I'd never had a baby, of course, and hadn't even seen one being born (except for those videos in our birthing class, which, by the way, were *nothing* like the real experience). Nonetheless, I couldn't shake the sense of emotional déjà vu. I didn't understand it, so I just let it go and allowed myself to get caught up in the incredible moment of newborn bliss.

She was born late in the afternoon on a Saturday. A little over 24 hours later, somewhere in the middle of Sunday night (probably the early morning hours of Monday), we were still in the hospital and I couldn't sleep. Honestly, with the excitement of the birth, the feeding, changing, and sleeping schedule of the new baby, and everything else that was happening, I wasn't all that interested in sleeping. Thankfully, both Michelle and Samantha were peacefully sleeping at that moment and I sat there watching them. I was feeling such joy, pride, contentment, and love as I looked at my beautiful new baby and my incredibly brave wife. I wanted to capture that moment, both for myself and also for Samantha, so I took out a piece of paper and started to write her a letter. My intention was to let her know exactly what it felt like just a day after her birth—and to reflect on my honest thoughts and feelings as a brand-new father, still buzzing from the whole experience.

The words flowed easily, which is often true for me, especially when I'm feeling an intense emotion. I let Samantha know about my love for her and all that entailed. I talked about the amazement of her birth and how in awe of her mommy I was. As I was in the midst of writing the letter, I started thinking about my own father, who had died a little more than four years earlier. I wondered what it felt like when he was a brand-new father. And I wondered how he would feel if he were here to meet his new granddaughter. I felt a deep sense of love and connection with my dad in that moment. I also felt a lot of empathy for him, given all of the struggles he'd experienced in his life. It was a beautiful moment of healing and connection for me with my dad—as a new dad myself—and with my sleeping baby girl.

I returned to the letter and began to write specifically about my father, her grandfather, whom she would never meet, but who I know would have loved to have met her. As I got a few sentences into writing to her about my dad, I dropped my pen and started sobbing. It hit me right then—the reason that the moment of Samantha's birth felt familiar to me was because it was very similar to the moment of my dad's death.

I'd had the honor of being in the room when my dad took his final breath, and although, obviously, the circumstances and emotions associated with my dad's death and Samantha's birth were quite different, there was something similarly sacred and beautiful about these two experiences. There was a presence and an energy in the room when Samantha came in and when my dad left. It was loving, safe, magical, and very much the same in both situations.

A great quote that is often attributed to Albert Einstein says, "There are only two ways to live your life. One is as though nothing is a miracle. The other is as though everything is a miracle." There is so much for us to be in awe of in life if we stop and pay attention. From the most profound to the merely mundane, life is full of wonder. Too often we take people and things for granted, instead of being amazed by the beauty and synchronicity that exists all around us.

When something "big" happens in life, like the birth of a child, the healing of an illness, a major achievement, a monumental peak experience, or something else we consider to be great, we often call it a miracle or at least give ourselves permission, albeit sometimes for just a very short time, to stop and appreciate the amazement of the specific event (and of life in general). This is wonderful and powerful when we do it. However, we don't have to wait for something "amazing" to happen to live with a sense of amazement. Even things that are challenging and painful can be amazing if we choose to look for the gifts in those experiences. Simple, positive things like sunsets, the laughter of children, the tress blowing in the wind, and even just the ability to walk are all things we could step back and appreci-ate, if we choose to do so.

Years ago a mentor of mine said, "Mike, if you want to dramatically change your life, there are two simple things you can do right now. Be easily impressed and hard to of-fend. Sadly, most of us have this the other way around. But if you can practice being authentically impressed and amazed by people, situations, and life itself, the way a child is, and make a firm commitment to yourself not to get offended unless something really big happens, you'll live a fantastic life."

The wisdom of this suggestion was profound. When we allow ourselves to be amazed by life, life is always amazing in return.

CHAPTER 32

Allow Things to Be Easy

A few years ago, I was in a cab on my way to JFK airport in New York, and I was lamenting to my friend Theo about how so many things seemed hard for me, and how some people just have things come so easy to them.

Theo stopped me in the middle of my rant and proceeded to call me out. "Mike," he said, "this 'story' you have about things being hard for you isn't really true. It seems to me that lots of things come pretty easy, you just make them hard by saying they are. What if you started actually owning that certain things come easy to you?"

As I heard him say this, I had a mixture of emotions and reactions. First of all, I felt grateful—I love having people in my life who are willing to call me out, even if my ego gets a little bent out of shape in the process. Second of all, I felt defensive and noticed that I wanted to justify myself against his challenge. Third of all, I felt a sense of fear and resistance to the idea of things coming easy to me.

As I thought about this more, I realized that my resistance to things being easy ran pretty deep, as I think it does for many people. Here are some of the main reasons I'd created and beliefs I'd held up to that point in my life to justify not allowing things to come easy:

- Easy means lazy.

- If things come easy to me, other people will get jealous, won't like me, and/or won't respect me.

- It doesn't really mean much if it comes easy.

- It's not fair for things to come easy to me—especially with so many people having such a hard time these days.

- I actually get off on struggling and suffering. I'm quite familiar with it and I've used it as motivation to change and "succeed" for much of my life.

- My ability to work hard, overcome adversity, and rise above challenges are all things my ego uses to feel superior to others.

- If I admit that something is easy for me, it will seem arrogant and then people will root for me to fail.

Maybe you can relate to some of these?

Getting in touch with some of these beliefs was painful and liberating at the same time. However, it did help me realize how ridiculous some of them were and how much of my energy I'd been giving away to them in the process.

It's almost like I was walking around worried that someone was going to say to me, "Mike, you have it so easy," and I was preparing my defensive responses: "Oh yeah, well let me tell you how hard I work, how challenging things are for me, and how much stuff I've had to overcome along the way." What's up with this? It's like I was preparing for a fight that didn't even exist. Do you ever do that?

While working hard and overcoming challenges aren't inherently bad, resisting ease and being attached to struggle causes us such a great deal of stress. And, in many cases, it's totally self-induced and unnecessary. As we also know from experience, what we focus on tends to manifest itself in our lives. Therefore, if we expect things to be hard, they more likely will be. And, on the flip side, if we expect them to be easy, that becomes more likely as well.

In the past few years since Theo and I had that conversation, I have been consciously expanding my capacity for things to be easier. Ironically, this isn't always easy for me, but I'm much more comfortable allowing things to go smoothly, and I continue to put my attention in this direction. Writing this book, in fact, has been much easier than I expected it to be and much easier than my two previous experiences of writing books. I caught myself a number of times thinking, *Wait a minute, this is too easy; it doesn't really count unless it's hard and I suffer.* As soon as I caught myself thinking this, I laughed at myself, noticed my tendency to make things hard unnecessarily, and challenged myself in a kind and loving way to allow it to be easy.

What if we simply allowed things to be easier in our lives? What if we started to speak about and own the aspects of our lives that are actually easy for us and even expected things to get easier? Easy doesn't mean lazy, that we aren't willing to work in a passionate way, or that we expect a free ride—it means that we're willing to have things work out. We trust that all is well and allow life to flow in a positive way.

Our desire and ability to embrace ease isn't selfish, arrogant, or unrealistic—it's profoundly optimistic (in an authentic way) and can actually enhance our ability to impact others. The more energy and attention we place on surviving, getting by, or even "striving" for success, the less available we are to make a difference for other people. Although it may seem counterintuitive to us, having things be easy is one of the best ways we can show up for those around us—both by our example and with our freed-up positive energy.

As Richard Bach famously wrote, "Argue for your limitations and you get to keep them." What if we stopped arguing on behalf of how "hard" things are, and started allowing our lives to be filled with peace and ease? While the idea of things being easy may not be, ironically, the easiest thing for you to embrace, I challenge you—as I continue to challenge myself—to take this on in your life and become more comfortable with it . . . maybe it'll be easier than you think!

CHAPTER 33

Accept Yourself

I had the honor of first meeting author Dr. Robert Holden when we both spoke at an event together last year. Robert is someone whom I've admired for quite some time. It was wonderful to get a chance to meet him in person and hear him speak live. In his talk, he said something that touched me: "There's no amount of self-improvement that can make up for a lack of self-acceptance."

This statement really resonated, and as I started to think about it more, I realized that so much of my life and my work is focused on self-improvement. And while there's nothing wrong with wanting to improve ourselves, too often we go about it erroneously, thinking that if we "achieve" the "improvement" we're after, we'll then feel good about ourselves. As Robert pointed out in his talk (and as most of us have experienced in our lives many times), it doesn't work this way.

We live in a culture that's obsessed with self-improvement. We turn on the TV, look at magazines, take classes, read books, listen to others, and surf the Web, and constantly get told that if we just fixed ourselves a bit, we'd be better off. How often do you find yourself thinking something like, *If I just (lost a little weight, made a little more money, improved my health, had more inspiring work, lived in a nicer place, fixed some of my flaws, improved my relationships), then I'd be happy?* Even though I know better, this type of thinking shows up inside my own head more often than I'd like.

I was on the road a few years ago in Washington, DC, and had lunch with my friend Sharon, whom I really admire—her passion, authenticity, and presence are infectious. She's dedicated her life to serving others and has had a very successful career in the nonprofit world. I'm grateful to know her and for her wisdom and perspective. When we got together that day for lunch, she said, "Mike, I've noticed something, especially in the past few years. Now that I'm in my fifties, I'm much more at peace with myself than ever before."

"Really?" I said. "Why do you think that is?"

"Well," she said, "for many years I spent a lot of time and energy trying to impress people. Constantly trying to live up to certain expectations often made me feel like I wasn't good enough. Even with all of the success I've had, a sense of real peace and confidence about myself had mostly eluded me." She continued, "However, in the past few years, I've just started to care a lot less about what other people think of me, and in the process have turned my attention to what I think about myself. And you know what? I like who and how I am—and don't want to waste any more of my precious time on this planet in judgment of myself or trying to live up to other people's standards."

I appreciated Sharon's self-awareness and her wisdom. Although I was not quite at the same stage or age in life, I could relate very much to what she was saying and where she was coming from. In the past few years, I've been focusing more on acceptance and less on improvement. One specific thing I've learned to accept about myself has to do with reading. I've never been a big reader, and for many years I carried around quite a bit of shame and embarrassment about it—like I was somehow a fraud as a writer. I also had been taught that being well-read is important, especially if you want to be smart and influential. When I finally admitted to myself, and started admitting to other people, that I don't like to read and much prefer to listen, it was pointed out to me that I'm probably an auditory learner. Turns out, I am. If I listen to someone speak, or listen to an audio book, not only is it much easier for me to pay attention, it's also easier for me to remember. Since realizing this, I've stopped judging myself for not reading and have simply chosen to get my books on audio, which I'm able to listen to on the road, while I work out, and more.

What if we gave ourselves permission to accept ourselves fully, right now? While this is a simple concept, it's one of the many things in life that's easier said than done. One of the biggest pieces of resistance we have regarding self-acceptance is that we erroneously think that by accepting ourselves, we may somehow be giving up, resigning ourselves to remain exactly as we are. But this isn't true. Acceptance is acceptance—it's about allowing things to be as they are, even if we don't like them. It doesn't mean you can't still work for change.

The paradox of self-acceptance is that when we allow ourselves to accept who we are, where we are, and what's really happening, we actually give ourselves the opportunity to make changes in our lives in a healthy way. When we obsess about and/or demand these changes *in order* to feel good about ourselves, it almost never works.

Most of the time it's our own self-criticism, perfection demands, and impatience that are actually getting in the way of what we truly want. Imagine if we changed our approach and just accepted ourselves exactly as we are in this moment!

CHAPTER 34

Be Real and Compassionate about Money

As I mentioned in the introduction to this book, 2009 was an extremely challenging year for both Michelle and me. Among the many issues we faced that year, one of the most painful was the difficult financial situation we'd put ourselves into: we were $105,000 in debt and about $300,000 upside down on our house by the end of that year. There were a number of factors that contributed to this, some of which had to do with the economic downturn and the collapse of the housing market, but more had to do with our lack of awareness, understanding, and responsibility with our money.

I grew up without a lot of money. My parents split up when I was three; it was 1977 and my mom hadn't worked much in the eight years since she had gotten pregnant with my sister, Lori. My dad made a decent living as a radio announcer, but with him gone, my mom was forced to take care of us, find work, and figure out how to navigate life as a single parent, which, as a Catholic girl from Rhode Island who didn't have any family in California, wasn't easy.

My dad, who had been pretty actively engaged in our lives the first five years after he and my mom split (we'd see him every other weekend), lost his job in late 1981 when his bipolar disorder got the best of him. We no longer saw him on a regular basis—he slipped into a very deep depression and stopped paying child support. My mom had recently started working for herself at that time as a wholesale sales rep for a few companies that made fashion accessories. She was trying to get her business off the ground so she could work for herself and have flexibility with her schedule. She was doing the best she could to raise us without much support from my dad—emotionally, practically, or financially.

One of the first and most poignant memories I have of realizing we didn't have a lot of money is of one night during a major rainstorm in February of 1982, just after my eighth birthday. The rain had gotten so intense that the ceiling in our living room started to leak. I remember initially thinking it was fun as my mom had Lori and me run into the kitchen to get some pots and pans and put them down on the floor to catch the water. In the midst of my laughter and excitement, I looked at my mom. It didn't seem like she was having much fun. All of a sudden, she fell to the floor and began to sob. Lori rushed over to her to comfort her, and I followed, confused by what was going on. She looked up at us through her tears and said, "I don't know what we're going to do." She then told us we didn't have the money to take care of the leaky roof on our house. My mom was scared and overwhelmed, and, in that moment, so was I.

Over the next few years, and throughout most of my childhood and adolescence, money (or lack thereof) became a major source of stress, worry, and disappointment in my family. I heard the words *we can't afford it* so often as a child that by the time I became a teenager, I mostly stopped asking for things. While my mom's business did grow a bit, we essentially lived hand to mouth, and it was hard. We had no savings, no college funds, and no financial plan of any kind. We didn't go on vacation, and when things around the house broke, they often weren't fixed or replaced. I was constantly aware of what many of my friends had and what they were able to do in comparison to me.

I got into Stanford and was able to go, thanks, in part, to my success in baseball and also to the enormous financial aid package I was offered. While I wasn't super focused on money, I definitely wanted to have a different and more abundant financial experience when I got older. I hoped one day I would be rich, and part of my motivation to make it to the major leagues was to dramatically change my financial reality. When I got drafted by the Kansas City Royals in 1995 after my junior year at Stanford, I received a $35,000 signing bonus. It was the first time in my life I actually had a little money of my own. I was elated, but also scared—not sure what to do with it. After buying a car and a few other things, paying my taxes, and trying to live on the very small amount of money I was paid in the minor leagues, most of that money was gone within a year. When my playing career ended just a few years later, without having made it to the big leagues or making much money, I was forced to figure out what to do with my life and how I would make money. I had no clue about either.

In the summer of 2004, after Michelle and I had been living together in San Francisco for two years, we got engaged. We were excited about getting married, although scared at the same time. Even though I was starting to make a little bit of money and my speaking and coaching business was gaining some momentum, we didn't have any money saved. In fact, we were both in debt and didn't have a financial plan at all. Even with our lean financial situation, given the economic climate at the time, we were pre-qualified for a $650,000 home loan and were told we could "buy" a house without having to put down any money, which is what we did in early 2005.

Although I didn't feel ready to buy a house and didn't think we were in a healthy financial position to do so (which, in hindsight, we weren't), my decision to go ahead with it was based almost completely on fear. I was scared that if we didn't buy a house at that time we'd get priced out of the market given how much home prices were going up. I was scared to disappoint Michelle because she really wanted a house as we were getting ready to get married and hoping to start a family. I was scared to admit my fear and to acknowledge that I didn't think I was ready for the responsibility of owning a home—both financially and energetically. I was scared to admit that I wasn't really sure how to make money, save money, combine my finances with Michelle's, and become the primary breadwinner for our family. My deepest fear was that I would continue my legacy of financial struggle and always live hand to mouth, since that was all I'd ever known.

Over the next few years, I did the best I could to pay the mortgage and all of our bills, expand my business, and provide for our family. Life was intense and exciting—two babies, two books, lots of travel, and an enormous amount of activity. Although things were going well and I was making a lot more money, we kept spending more to keep up with our expanding life and my expanding business. I felt a great deal of pressure and things felt out of control, financially and otherwise. We didn't have a plan and I still didn't feel like I knew what I was doing, but there didn't seem to be time to slow down to think about it, talk about it, or do anything about it. I figured if I just kept making more money, it would all work out.

Then 2009 happened. Not only did I lose a great deal of work to the economic meltdown (many of my corporate clients canceled their events and cut their training budgets), I also invested a lot of money into my business and the launch of my second book. The timing was terrible for us, and by the end of that year we found ourselves in a real mess. And while it didn't happen overnight, we were humbled by how quickly it seemed like we had put ourselves in such a hole, baffled by how we got there, and totally confused about how to get ourselves out. It felt eerily similar to that moment when I was eight, on the floor with my mom and sister surrounded by pots and pans.

Somewhat miraculously, less than two years later, we were completely debt-free, out from under the weight of our house situation, and on track in a positive direction with our finances. How we were able to do this was based on a variety of things. And while there were a lot of practical things we did and there was a lot of hard work involved on our part, the two most important things we did were on a personal and internal level: we learned to get real and to have compassion for ourselves.

Getting real wasn't fun or easy, especially at first, and it was quite humbling. We had to look at the reality of where we were, get specific about the numbers themselves, and investigate how we'd gotten there in the first place. Basically, we'd consistently spent more money than we'd made for many years. We also had not done a very good job planning or tracking our finances, which seemed increasingly complicated for us now that we had a family of four, a house, and lots of new expenses, as well as a business that generated significantly inconsistent amounts of income and required large chunks of money to be spent at certain times.

We started talking about our situation, in detail, to each other and to a few important people close to us. We told them about our debt, our house, and our specific challenges. We did this with people we felt we could trust and who might be able to help. It felt scary, embarrassing, and vulnerable, but at the same time, also liberating and empowering. Getting real like this forced us to "sober up," start taking a deeper level of responsibility, and begin the process of turning things around financially.

We also did our best to have compassion for ourselves and to look for the gifts in the situation. More difficult even than the specifics of what we were facing financially was the emotional impact. Both of us were dealing with an enormous amount of shame, embarrassment, guilt, and more. Michelle felt guilty that she had been so adamant about us buying our house when we did, which in hindsight we realized was one of the key factors that caused the mess we were in. She also felt a certain degree of helplessness due to the fact that she was at home taking care of the girls and couldn't directly impact our income. I, on the other hand, felt like a loser and blamed myself for our being in this bad of a spot. I clearly wasn't making enough money and since that was one of my primary responsibilities in our family, I felt embarrassed and like I was letting down Michelle and the girls big-time.

We both realized that the harsh judgments we had about ourselves, which we would sometimes project onto each other, were not only harmful but also were making a difficult situation even worse. We each dug deep in search of self-compassion, did our best to forgive ourselves and each other, and made a commitment to continually look for the "gifts" from what we were going through. We both did a lot of inner forgiveness work, in addition to outward practical work (with coaches, mentors, and others), that helped lead not only to our financial turnaround, but to our personal healing as well.

Money is one of the most emotionally charged issues we contend with, especially these days. Many of us have some real baggage about money that we bring with us into our relationships, our work, and most aspects of our lives. And, because of our feelings of shame, guilt, confusion, judgment, fear, arrogance, and embarrassment about money, we often don't talk about it in a real way. Our lack of comfort with authentic discussions about money is one of the biggest reasons it continues to be such a source of stress and confusion for so many of us. We also tend to be very secretive about money. As the saying goes, "We're only as sick as our secrets."

CHAPTER 35

Stop Should-ing on Yourself

In a session a while back, my counselor Eleanor said to me, "Mike, it sounds like you're should-ing all over yourself." I laughed when she said this, as I've heard this expression many times before—I've even given this same feedback to others. However, something about her saying this to me at that particular moment caught my attention.

As I started to take inventory of the most important aspects of my life, I was a bit shocked to realize that much of my motivation in these areas comes from the perspective of what I think I *should* do, say, or feel, and not from a place of what's authentic and true for me.

Most specifically, I find myself challenged by various competing "shoulds" in my head in regard to my business and my family. Both require quite a bit of energy, which is true for most of us. Because I run my own business, I have to make a lot of choices about where to focus my time and energy—writing, traveling to speak, staying home with my family, and so on. The choices I make have a big impact on my family not only because I'm the primary breadwinner but also because they determine how much I'll be around to help with day-to-day life. I try to be as mindful as I can about these choices, although it isn't always easy. If I'm not conscious about it, that voice in my head can easily pop up and say "You *should* be spending more time with your family" when I'm on the road speaking or up early (or late) working on a project. At other times, that voice can start talking when I'm on vacation with my family, at an event at the girls' school, or even playing a game with one of them: "What are you doing? You *should* be working right now, so you can send these girls to college and make more money for your family."

Our obsession with doing, saying, or feeling the way we think we *should* is actually less about genuine desire or commitment, and more about a lack of self-trust. When we operate from that place of *should*, it's often because we're feeling scared, flawed, or simply not confident in our own thoughts and beliefs. This insecurity leads us to look outside of ourselves for guidance, and this often causes us even more stress.

What if instead of asking ourselves "What should I do?" we asked different, more empowering questions like, "What's true for me?" or "What am I committed to?" or "What do I really want?" These questions, and others like them, come from a much deeper place of authenticity.

This is not to say that everything we think we *should* do is inherently bad. That is clearly not the case. Some things we think we *should* do—like eat better, communicate with kindness, exercise, try new things, organize our lives, take care of ourselves, and so much more—can be important aspects of our success and well-being (as well as that of those around us).

However, when we come from a place of *should,* our motivation and underlying intention for doing something is compromised—even if it's something we consider to be positive or healthy. In other words, we often feel stressed, bitter, resentful, or annoyed when we're motivated by *should*. This "should" mentality is based on an erroneous notion that there is some big book of rules we must follow in order to be happy and successful. There are times, unfortunately, when I'm doing something "fun" like riding bikes with my girls, watching a movie with Michelle, or going to a ball game with some buddies, but my obsession with what else I "should" be doing takes me away from fully enjoying and appreciating the experience in the moment.

The distinction here is one of obligation versus choice; "have to" versus "want to." When we stop should-ing on ourselves, we're less motivated by fear and can choose to be inspired by authentic desire.

Sometimes we may also find ourselves looking to others to tell us what we "should" do. While there's nothing wrong with our seeking guidance, our deepest truths come from within. When we let go of our insatiable desire to figure out what we "should" do, we give ourselves permission to listen to our inner wisdom, trust ourselves, and make whatever changes we deem to be important. And, if there are actions we want to take that we believe will enhance our experience of life, we can take them from a place of self-trust. There are so many new and exciting possibilities we can create once we let go of "should."

CHAPTER 36

Take Good Care of You

I was at an event in San Francisco a few years ago and had the privilege of spending some time with Louise Hay, founder of Hay House and best-selling author of *You Can Heal Your Life*. Louise is someone I've admired for a long time—she's a true pioneer in the world of personal development. It was an honor for me to connect with her at this event.

On the final day of the conference, I asked Louise if she was planning to fly home (back to San Diego, just an hour's flight from San Francisco) that evening. She said, "Oh no, Mike, I would never do that to myself." Her response, while simple, floored me. I thought, *Wow, what a great example of honoring and caring for yourself*. Then I thought, *I could use more of that*.

At that time, I was feeling run down, exhausted, and overwhelmed by my life. Our girls were four and one, I was traveling quite a bit, and I felt like I couldn't keep up with everything. My schedule was packed with so many activities, I felt like it was hard for me to breathe, much less enjoy what I was doing. I also felt like a victim of my "crazy" schedule and life, which gave me a built-in excuse for not showing up for others or taking full responsibility for my actions (i.e., "What do you want from me? Do you have any idea how much I have going on right now?").

Around this same time, I was reading a wonderful book called *The Art of Extreme Self-Care*, by Cheryl Richardson. In this book, Cheryl challenges us to make our self-care a top priority. I loved the book, and while the concepts were fairly simple, familiar, and straightforward, I felt a great deal of resistance as I started to practice some of what Cheryl was saying.

Unfortunately, a lot of us think of self-care as selfish or as something we should do when we get everything else done. I would find myself thinking, *Once I take care of all the important people and things in my life, then I'll take care of myself.* In addition to this, I also think we can sometimes be motivated to take care of ourselves out of fear or guilt: *I should eat better. I should exercise more. I'm not taking good care of myself and if I keep this up I'm going to gain weight, get sick, or something really bad is going to happen to me.* These types of negative, critical thoughts often roll around in our brains, and often are the impetus or motivation for us to "take care of ourselves."

Authentic self-care is not selfish and it's not a guarantee that we won't gain weight or get sick—although taking care of ourselves would probably make those things less likely. True self-care is about honoring ourselves, caring for ourselves, nurturing ourselves, and loving ourselves—both for our own benefit and for the benefit of everyone around us.

I saw Dr. Andrew Weil on *Larry King Live* a number of years ago. Dr. Weil, who had been a leader in the field of alternative medicine for decades, was talking to Larry about the importance of self-care. He mentioned that there is a great model for this in the human body—the heart. Dr. Weil said, "Each time the heart beats, it first pumps blood to itself, then to the rest of the body. It has to work this way in order for us to stay alive." He continued, "The same is true for us as human beings. We have to take care of ourselves first, so we can take care of others."

Self-care is fundamental to not only our personal well-being but also to our relationships with the people closest to us. It empowers us to be more available and generous with the people around us in an authentic way, while modeling to them how we want to be treated. As Michael Bernard Beckwith says, "The Golden Rule is 'Do unto others as you would have them do unto you.' The Platinum Rule is 'How I treat myself is training others how to treat me.'"

At the beginning of 2012, Michelle and I made a commitment to take even better care of ourselves in service of our marriage, our girls, and our lives. One of the practical steps we took was to start a new exercise and eating program called The Happy Body, based on a book and program we'd heard about with the same title. The program consisted of eating a primarily paleo diet, which is lots of vegetables and protein, and eating at particular times throughout the day—essentially every three hours. It also involved a daily 45-minute workout we could do at home and a 5-minute meditation right after the workout.

The details of the program, both eating and exercise, were fairly simple and straightforward. We were excited to start the program and do it together. In addition to this, right around the same time, I began working with my counselor Eleanor. In our very first session, she challenged me to focus on taking care of myself and fulfilling my own needs—not looking outside myself for approval and achievement to fill me up.

By the end of February of 2012, I'd lost 25 pounds. And while the weight loss was exciting, what was most exciting to me was the enhanced energy and vitality I felt. As great as the specific techniques were, I actually think the reason

I felt so good had less to do with the details of what I was doing and more to do with my commitment to making self-care a priority. Taking care of myself was something I'd done before, of course, but was something I often struggled with on many levels, especially in terms of making it a consistent priority in my life. However, through this process, something shifted inside of me and I began to realize the importance of self-care at an even deeper level.

Over the past few years, I've continued to use the techniques that jump-started my practice. And while my consistency does ebb and flow, I continue to feel the benefits of my commitment to self-care. I am energized physically and have kept off most of the weight I lost. I have noticed that I treat myself better, have more compassion for myself, and find it easier to prioritize my well-being and myself in general. And this has led to more peace and more confidence in my life.

Taking care of ourselves takes courage, commitment, and willingness. Given the nature of our busy lives, it's not so easy, logistically or emotionally, for us to make and keep our self-care commitments. It's not about doing it "right" or "perfectly," or even about following some detailed plan to a tee. It's simply about remembering that we deserve to take care of ourselves, and when we do, it not only nourishes us but also allows us to be available for important things and people in our lives.

CHAPTER 37

Focus on What You Can Control

In April of 1995 we had a meeting in our Stanford base-ball locker room with our pitching coach, Dean Stotz, and our entire pitching staff (about 18 guys, half of the whole team) that had a profound impact on me. At that point in the season, we were really struggling. Going into the year, we were the number one–ranked team in the country. According to all the experts, we were supposed to have the best team in college baseball. But, as we say in sports, you don't play the games on paper. As the season had gotten under way, we lost some key games and had some significant injuries. By April, which was the midway point of the season, we were no longer ranked number one in the country. In fact, we'd fallen out of the national rankings completely.

Coach Stotz, sensing our frustration and experiencing some of his own, decided to have a conversation with us in the locker room to see if we could shift things in a more positive direction. He said to all of us, "Look, guys, I know it's been tough and we haven't been playing that well. I wanted to get together as a pitching staff and talk about what's been going on. Instead of me doing all the talking, I want to hear from you guys." He continued, "Let's have an

open, honest discussion about some of your biggest frustra-
tions. You have permission to say anything you want."

Although we were a little nervous, especially at first,
once we started talking, we began to open up and Coach
Stotz started writing down what we were saying on the
whiteboard in the locker room. Many of the things we
talked about initially were pretty straightforward baseball-
related issues—we weren't scoring enough runs, we weren't
playing great defense, we'd blown a couple of games that
we all thought we should have won. Some of the stuff had
more to do with some specific circumstances we'd been
facing: the injuries, the rainy weather early in the season
that caused some games to be canceled or rescheduled,
the ongoing construction at our stadium that had been de-
layed by the weather, a few questionable calls from umpires
that cost us a game or two. After a while, some of the guys
were willing to get a little more personal and started talking
about some even more sensitive subjects, like playing time
(thinking they weren't getting a fair chance to play), team
policies and rules they didn't like, and even some of the attitudes of the other members of our team who weren't in
the room (there is often tension on a baseball team between
the pitchers and position players, and that was definitely the
case on our team).

Coach Stotz didn't say much, he just continued to add
to what was now becoming a pretty long list. When we
were finally done, he said, "Look, men, I understand your
frustration. I feel the same way about a lot of these things
and there aren't very many things up on this board that
I would even disagree with. But, I have a very simple yet
important question to ask you—how many of the things on
this list can you control?"

As I stared at the list and contemplated Coach Stotz's question, I realized that most of the things up on the board were clearly out of my control. They were all based on what other people were doing or not doing, or based on circumstances that weren't up to me. One of my teammates raised his hand and said, "I don't think there's anything up on that board we can fully control."

Coach Stotz then said, "That's right! The truth is, most of these things are just complaints. And while there may be some validity to them, the more important thing to remember is that there are really only three things that you can control in baseball, and in life, for that matter. Those three things are your attitude, your effort, and your perspective. That's it—attitude, effort, and perspective. If you can focus your attention on those three things—have your attitude be as positive as it can be, your effort as passionate as possible, and your perspective as healthy as you're able, then you can be a productive member of this pitching staff and ultimately of this team. The same is true for life. Remembering these things will help you engage effectively in anything that happens."

For me sitting there in that locker room at the age of 21, it was a pivotal moment and a profound insight about how I could relate to not only baseball but my life moving forward. I was grateful for those words of wisdom. They also seemed to have a positive impact on our team, as we did turn things around that season and ended up making it to the College World Series, which was a huge thrill for all of us.

I've thought about that conversation many times over the past 19 years and have shared that same insight with many of my clients. Too often we get caught up in focusing on things we can't control and render ourselves ineffective at both influencing positive change and enjoying the experience.

Remembering that we have complete control over our attitude, effort, and perspective is empowering—especially when we find ourselves worried about how things are going to turn out with a particular project, relationship, goal, or any other important aspect of our lives, big or small. We can be incredibly powerful and effective in our ability to create and manifest the things we want in our lives, especially when we focus on what we can actually control.

CHAPTER 38

Forgive Yourself

In December of 2011, I decided to head up to Calistoga for a few days. Calistoga is a small town in Napa Valley, about an hour from where we live. For the past few years, Michelle and I have each gone up there occasionally by ourselves for some personal retreat time. It's been a great self-care practice that has benefited us both individually and as a family. It's amazing how taking just a few days away can help me put things in perspective, recharge, and reconnect to what's most important in my life.

That December was an emotional time for me. It was the end of what had been a tumultuous year, filled with big highs and big lows. My mom had died in June, we did the short sale on our house in August and moved, and life had changed for us in many significant ways. Even with the difficulty and intensity of the year, a lot of really good things had happened, too. It felt like life was moving in a really positive direction for us.

As I took some time to reflect and go within, I realized I was carrying around an enormous amount of resentment, most of which was directed at myself. I took with me to Calistoga some old cassette tapes of an audio program called "Forgiving Yourself," which I'd actually never listened to when I'd purchased it many years before. The tapes talked about being hard on ourselves, and being critical and harboring resentment toward ourselves—all things that I'd done quite a bit throughout my life. Based on the suggestions of this audio program and my own insight and awareness, I spent a lot of time over the course of those few days writing in my journal and meditating, all with the specific intention of forgiving myself.

I started to write down a long list of things that I wanted to forgive myself for—being harsh and critical of some of the people closest to me, being annoyed and unkind to my girls at times, worrying about all kinds of superficial things, doing harm to my body over the years, not taking good care of myself, making mistakes in my business and with our finances, not practicing what I preached in my work, and on and on the list went.

As I wrote these things down in my journal, initially I was concerned that it was simply just my gremlin taking over and listing out all the things that were "wrong" with me and all the reasons why I was "bad." But as I allowed myself to engage more deeply in the process, I realized that what I was doing was simply telling the truth about all the things I'd been judging myself for. This was my attempt in some way to let go of the resentment I was holding toward myself. I was trying to move into a place of forgiveness and, ultimately, freedom. And while I wasn't sure if I knew exactly the "right" way to forgive myself, I decided to simply ask, in my writings, my prayers, and my meditations, to be forgiven. Before I went to bed at night, I would ask for the weight of this self-criticism and negativity to be lifted off of me.

By the time I left Calistoga, just a few days later, I felt 50 pounds lighter. Just a few weeks after that, I had my very first session with my counselor Eleanor. As Eleanor and I began to work together, which we've continued to do over the last few years with wonderful results, she began to explain to me the nature of growth and change.

"Mike, as you grow, change, and evolve, here are the basic steps involved in the process: recognize, acknowledge, forgive, and change. First," she said, "you must *recognize* what's going on and what you're doing. This is about seeing and about authentic awareness. Then you *acknowledge* the impact of what you're doing with compassion and without judgment. This is about feeling your emotions and owning the impact. Then," she said, "the most important step in the process is forgiveness—a willingness to *forgive* yourself. Self-forgiveness isn't about letting yourself off the hook, it's about caring enough to take a deeper level of responsibility. And when you do that, you're able to forgive yourself authentically. The fourth step," she continued, "is *change*. However, if you genuinely recognize, acknowledge, and forgive, the change pretty much happens on its own, and you don't have to—nor do you get to—control it. Change is the result of authentic forgiveness and authentic forgiveness is about releasing the past and all the stories you have associated with it." Then she followed up with the kicker: "Unfortunately, what you often do, Mike, and this is true for many people, is recognize, acknowledge, *punish*, and *repeat*—instead of forgive and change—which keeps certain negative patterns in place in your life and causes you a great deal of pain and suffering."

The truth of what Eleanor taught me resonated deeply and we continue to talk about it in our sessions today. Since that initial conversation, I've been consciously focused on forgiving myself as well as releasing the past and all of the stories I have connected to it. Given that I've got many years of experience of *not* doing this and still have a tendency to be hypercritical of myself, as many of us do, self-forgiveness continues to be a challenge for me, although it's getting easier. It's a practice, and like any practice, the more we do it, the easier it is and the more effective we become.

The more willing we are to take an honest look within—to recognize and acknowledge our self-sabotaging ways and to forgive ourselves for them—the more likely we can begin to change in an authentic and powerful way. Self-forgiveness makes it possible for us to forgive others and to live our lives with a genuine sense of freedom, peace, and love.

CHAPTER 39

Let Your Light Shine

In October of 2000, I had the opportunity to meet Dan Millman. Dan's classic book *Way of the Peaceful Warrior* had a profound impact on me and my life when I read it just a few years earlier. I was grateful to get a chance to connect with Dan and excited to gain some wisdom and insight from him as I attempted to start my business as a speaker and a coach, and hopefully, one day, become an author like him.

I said, "Dan, as excited and passionate as I am about the idea of helping and inspiring people, every time I think about speaking or writing, I worry that all my ideas are re-cycled from someone or somewhere else. I'm not sure I have any original ideas."

Dan said, "Mike, don't worry, everyone feels like that, especially when they're just starting out. It's my belief that there's only one light but many lamps. Your job is to simply shine your light as bright as possible, and trust that the people you are supposed to reach will resonate with you." I was grateful for the simplicity and wisdom of Dan's feedback, and I took it to heart.

Shining our light is something most of us want to do in life, but sometimes it can be a little tricky. As Marianne Williamson famously says in her book *A Return to Love*, "It is our light, not our darkness, that most frightens us." As much as we want to "shine," we often don't allow ourselves to do so, either because we don't think we deserve to or because we don't know how to handle it when we do. For many of us, it's much easier to struggle and suffer than it is to shine.

How about you? How do you feel when things go well for you? Are you comfortable shining? If you're anything like me, you may have some mixed feelings about it, as odd as that seems. While I do love it when things go well, I also notice that sometimes it poses certain challenges for me.

When things go really well in my life, as much as I appreciate and enjoy it, I also find myself feeling uncomfortable at the same time. Why is this? For me—and for many other folks—there are a few main reasons, as I noted in the earlier chapter, "Allow Things to Be Easy."

First, we may hear that voice in our head that says, *It's too good to be true,* or *It won't last,* or *You'll mess it up.* This, of course, is one of the sneaky ways our gremlin tries to rob us of our power and joy. Our gremlin convinces us not to shine too brightly, because if we do, we will have farther to fall when we fail.

Second, we worry that people won't like us, will judge us, or will get jealous of our success, power, or happiness, and thus pull away from us. Connected to this feeling of separation, we may also find ourselves worrying that if things go too well, people won't be able to relate to us. We may have picked up some of these beliefs in childhood or adolescence—from siblings, friends, or other kids in school. Many of us grew up in environments where we were constantly competing with and being compared to the people close to us. And, as much as we may have wanted to stand out, we also may have learned the hard way that there can be negative consequences for shining too brightly.

Third, much of our learning, growth, and evolution in life has come through pain and suffering. Even though we may have heard a number of teachers and mentors say that we can grow more effectively and elegantly through joy and love, sometimes we find ourselves worrying that if things get too good, we'll get lazy. We'll stop actively learning or somehow abandon our journey of personal growth.

Finally, we sometimes don't feel worthy of our success. It's as though we take our gifts, talents, and successes for granted, choosing to focus on all of the areas we think we need to improve, and in the process discount ourselves.

These and other limiting thoughts, attitudes, and beliefs have gotten in my way in the past. They've kept me stuck in difficult situations, or, at the very least, have limited my experience of joy and fulfillment. It's almost as if I've been more comfortable suffering than I have been when things were going well. When there are problems to deal with, I'm able to dig down deep, access my power, and rise up to meet them.

Your version of this may look a little different from mine, but lots of people I know and work with, even those who have created a lot of outward "success" in their lives, seem to struggle to some degree with allowing themselves to shine.

We all have this ability. We are born with it but somehow unlearn it as we grow. One of the most remarkable memories I have was as a brand-new father taking Samantha out in public for the very first time. After we brought her home from the hospital, we kept her in the house for the first few weeks, with the exception of visits to the doctor. She'd been born a little early, and had jaundice (which many babies born early do), and as new parents we were a little on the paranoid side, so we didn't feel comfortable taking her out in public. After about three weeks, we decided it was time, and, on the way home from the doctor one afternoon, we stopped at the store to pick up a few things.

Samantha was asleep in her car seat. I took her out, wrapped her up in a tight swaddle, and decided to carry her into the store in my arms. I had no idea what was about to occur. We walked through the front door and almost immediately I became the most popular guy there. People came running up to us to see the new baby. You often get a lot of attention when you're out with a baby, but when you go out with a newborn, it's even more intense—people are both excited and shocked to see such a tiny human being. I think that's because even those of us who've had babies forget how little they are when they first come out.

What felt like hordes of people came over to see Samantha, to congratulate us, and to whisper to her. They said things like, "Oh, look how beautiful you are," or "Welcome to Earth," or "You're amazing!" They said these things in a hushed tone (because she was asleep), but with such appreciation, authenticity, and reverence that I was stunned!

As we walked out of the store, amazed by what we'd just experienced, I said to Michelle, "That was incredible. But, it's so interesting that Samantha got all of that attention and appreciation—she didn't even do anything to deserve it. You're the one who carried her for all those months and gave birth to her, but no one even said anything about that. She just slept in my arms . . . and did nothing."

Even if she had been awake, Samantha, as a new baby, would probably not have consciously known what people were saying to her and about her, but she most likely would have been able to feel it, and would not have had any resistance to receiving that appreciation and attention. Unfortunately, as we get older, we pick up certain ideas and beliefs about what we deserve and don't deserve. Many of us learn, sadly, to dim our light based on our own fear or judgment (or that of those around us). But Samantha just lay there and let her light shine.

We don't have to dim our light. As Marianne Williamson also says later in that same famous passage from *A Return to Love*, "There's nothing enlightened about shrinking so that other people won't feel insecure around you." As we get more in touch with who we really are and let go of our fear of what other people think of us, we give ourselves permission to let our light shine brightly. And, when we do this, it can liberate us and inspire others.

CHAPTER 40

Live Like You're Going to Die (Because You Are)

On Friday, March 11, 2011, I picked up my mom at her house and we drove to the Kaiser Permanente Medical Center in downtown Oakland for the second time that week. The previous Friday, my mom had called me early in the morning to say she'd had a rough night of sleep because her back was really bothering her. I encouraged her to go get it checked out, and she'd gone in for an exam and an X-ray. The X-ray showed a spot on her lung, so they asked her to come back the following Monday for a CT scan. This Friday appointment was to follow up and get the results from the scan.

My mom, my sister Lori, and I had spent a lot of time together at Kaiser over the past year, as my mom had been diagnosed with early stage breast cancer the previous spring. She'd had two surgeries as well as radiation treatment that she'd just recently completed. The surgeries and treatment had been successful, and my mom was declared cancer-free. Her breast cancer ordeal had been quite scary and stressful for everyone. The doctor we were scheduled to meet with that Friday was the same oncologist she'd been seeing for the past year.

He walked into the room with an intensely somber look on his face and didn't make eye contact with us (although that was pretty normal for him). After a moment, he sat down and then said, "I'm sorry, Lois. I have some very bad news. Your CT scan has confirmed what we feared when we saw your X-ray. You have stage four lung cancer." The blood in my body turned ice-cold. I looked at my mom. I could see the terror and disbelief on her face. I moved across the room to where she was sitting and grabbed her hand. Neither of us said anything, nor did the doctor. The three of us just sat there in silence as his words hung in the air. I finally was able to utter, "What does this mean exactly?" He said, "Well, as you know, stage four is the most advanced. It looks as though the disease has spread significantly and aggressively. Unfortunately, there aren't many medical options. We won't be able to operate. You can choose to pursue treatment options like chemotherapy and radiation, but with your advanced disease, we're not sure if the benefits of that outweigh the costs. That's a choice you'll have to make in the coming days; it really comes down to a quality-of-life issue." After another long pause, my mom asked, in a bit of a hushed tone, "How much time do you think I have?"

"Well," he said, "based on the advanced nature of your disease, it's hard to say for sure. On average with stage four lung cancer, we're looking at a year, possibly less." There really wasn't much else to say or ask at that point. After another long and intense period of silence, the doctor got up, shook my hand, patted my mom on the shoulder, and said, "I'm very sorry, Lois." I think he said a few other things after that—instructions about the next appointment or something. Quite frankly, I really don't remember; it was all a bit of a blur. When he walked out of the room, however, my mom collapsed into my arms, sobbing. While I'd seen my mother cry a number of times throughout my life, although it wasn't common, this, of course, was still like nothing I'd ever experienced. Not even her breast cancer diagnosis brought on this kind of emotion. This diagnosis felt different and final; she'd just been told she was going to die.

A few weeks later as the reality of the situation had set in and my mom began to get quite sick, I was on a run one morning and thought, *I wonder what it's like to be my mom right now, knowing she's going to die.* As soon as I had that thought, I literally stopped running and then thought, *Wait a minute, I know I'm going to die, too—I just don't know when.*

As simple as this thought was, it was profound for me. I don't live my life all that consciously aware of my own death—even though I know it's inevitable. My own fears about death—my own and the deaths of people close to me—often force me to avoid thinking about it altogether. I do catch myself worrying about dying, sometimes more often than I'd like to admit, especially with our girls being as young as they are and given how many people close to me have died in the past decade or so.

I also hesitate to talk about death because it seems like such a morbid topic, a real downer. I worry that it's too intense to address, or I superstitiously fear that if I focus on death I will somehow attract it to me or to those around me.

As a culture, we don't really talk about death or deal with it in a meaningful way since it can be quite scary, emotional, and painful. Death also seems like the exact opposite of so much of what we do obsess about—youth, productivity, vitality, results, beauty, improvement, the future, and so on.

But what if we embraced death, talked about it more, and shared our own thoughts, feelings, and questions about it? While for some of us this may seem uncomfortable, undesirable, or even a little weird, think how liberating it would be to face the reality of death directly.

Steve Jobs gave a powerful and famous commencement speech at Stanford's graduation in 2005 entitled "How to Live Before You Die." In that speech, which now has even more poignancy given that he has passed away, Steve said, "Remembering that you are going to die is the best way I know to avoid the trap of thinking you have something to lose. You are already naked. There is no reason not to follow your heart."

Contemplating death in a conscious way doesn't have to freak us out. Knowing that our human experience is limited and that at some mysterious point in the future our physical body will die is both sobering and liberating.

The reason I've always appreciated memorial services—even when I've been in deep pain and grief over the death of someone close to me—is because there is a powerful consciousness that often surrounds death. When someone passes away, we feel more like we have permission to get real and be vulnerable, so we can focus on what's most important (not the ego-based fear, comparison, and self-criticism that often run our lives).

What if we tapped into this empowering awareness all the time—not just because someone close to us dies or because we have our own near-death experience? What if we instead choose to affirm life and appreciate the blessings, gifts, and opportunities that it provides? As I heard in a great workshop I took years ago, "Most of you are trying to survive life; you have to remember that no one ever has."

My mom's illness and her death, just three months after diagnosis, were painful but powerful reminders of the precious and temporary nature of human life. There are reminders of this everywhere; we just often choose to avoid them, deny them, or worry about them—instead of embracing them.

I decided to end the book with this chapter on living like you're going to die for a few reasons. First of all, it brings things back full circle to the first chapter, "Focus on What Truly Matters," in which I talked about both the pain and the beauty of my mom's death, and all that I learned from her as she was dying. Second of all, the awareness and perspective we often gain in the face of death is directly related to the core themes of this book— go for it, be yourself, accept who you are, be gentle with yourself, have the courage to be vulnerable, love yourself, remember that you are the source of your own happiness, and practice completely embracing and surrendering to the present moment.

Living like we're going to die is actually about remembering to fully engage in life *right now*, to be grateful for the precious gift that it is, and to take back our power from anywhere and everywhere we give it away. We're much stronger, more beautiful, more powerful, and more capable than we often give ourselves credit for. As we continue to catch ourselves—with empathy—when we stray off course, discount ourselves, and focus on things that don't really matter, we can bring ourselves back to the truth of who we are. We can remind ourselves that we're magnificent, valuable, and lovable just the way we are.

Thank you for taking this journey with me. I feel honored, humbled, and grateful to have been able to connect with you this way, and I hope you found this book useful.

If you'd like to connect with me personally, get more information about my work, attend one of my events, bring me in to speak to your group, and/or utilize the resources on my website, feel free to visit www.Mike-Robbins.com.

You can also connect with me on Facebook, www.facebook.com/mikerobbinspage, and Twitter, @MikeDRobbins.

Appendix

MEDITATIONS

In the book, I speak about two meditations that have been very beneficial in my life: the Fulfilling Your Own Needs meditation and the Embracing Powerlessness meditation. Below, you will find instructions for both of them.

FULFILLING YOUR OWN NEEDS

- Find a comfortable position—either sitting or lying down—and allow yourself to relax with your eyes closed. I often do this in bed in the morning, lying down.

- Once you are relaxed, imagine in your mind that you are in a safe and comfortable place.

- Visualize or imagine a big sphere of light in front of you—and inside of the sphere, there are seven chambers, one for each of these seven needs: safety, security, belonging/value, love, knowing, beauty, and spirituality.

- Step inside of the first chamber (safety) and stay there until you feel the feeling of that need at a deep emotional level.

- Next, step into each of the other chambers around the sphere (one at a time, in order), with the seventh and final chamber (spirituality) located in the middle of the sphere itself. As you step into each chamber, stay inside that particular chamber until you get a deep sense of the feeling associated with that specific need before moving on to the next one. When you get to that seventh chamber, stay there in the center of the sphere as long as you'd like—it can be a great place to focus on what you'd like to create, experience, and manifest into your life. (Allow yourself to visualize that.)

- When you are finished, step out of the seventh chamber and the entire sphere, back into that same safe and comfortable place where you started. Then, allow your eyes to open gently.

You can do this meditation as often as you like and for as long as you like. I usually do it for close to 30 minutes, but sometimes much shorter, and sometimes even longer. If you would like to be guided through this meditation, please download the free audio recording from my website at www.Mike-Robbins.com/meditations.

Embracing Powerlessness

- Find a comfortable position—either sitting or lying down—and allow yourself to relax with your eyes closed. I often do this in bed in the morning, lying down.

- Once you are relaxed, imagine yourself lying down in a field of soft grass.

- As you relax into the grass, feel the ground beneath you turn to water, and allow yourself to sink down a bit, and float on top of the surface . . . then let go and allow the water to support you and your relaxation completely.

- As you are floating on the water, say to yourself, "I give myself permission to *feel* powerless. Just because I *feel* powerless, doesn't mean I *am* powerless." Keep repeating this mantra to yourself as you allow yourself to float on your back with the water supporting you.

- Once you have allowed yourself to fully experience and embrace the *feeling* of powerlessness, imagine that the watery ground turns solid again, and allow yourself to lie there in the field of soft grass for a moment. You can then gently open your eyes and come out of the meditation/visualization.

You can do this meditation as often as you'd like and for as long as you'd like. I usually do it for about 10 or 15 minutes.

You can also use this same meditative process for any emotion (e.g., fear, anger, sadness, jealousy, rage, shame, hurt); just replace the word and feeling in the mantra. For example, "I give myself permission to *feel* scared. Just because I *feel* scared, doesn't mean I *am* scared."

If you would like to be guided through this meditation, please download the free audio recording from my website at www.Mike-Robbins.com/meditations.

Resources

Below you'll find a list of resources (books, workshops, and videos) that I believe in and recommend strongly. Each of them will support and empower you on your path of growth.

Books

Carry On, Warrior: Thoughts on Life Unarmed, by Glennon Melton

Daring Greatly: How the Courage to Be Vulnerable Transforms the Way We Live, Love, Parent, and Lead, by Brené Brown

The Dark Side of the Light Chasers: Reclaiming Your Power, Creativity, Brilliance, and Dreams, by Debbie Ford

Don't Sweat the Small Stuff . . . and It's All Small Stuff: Simple Ways to Keep the Little Things from Taking Over Your Life, by Richard Carlson

Dying to Be Me: My Journey from Cancer, to Near Death, to True Healing, by Anita Moorjani

Emotional Equations: Simple Steps for Creating Happiness + Success in Business + Life, by Chip Conley

Enjoy Every Sandwich: Living Each Day as if It Were Your Last, by Lee Lipsenthal

Feel the Fear and Do It Anyway: Dynamic Techniques for Turning Fear, Indecision, and Anger into Power, Action, and Love, by Susan Jeffers

Five Wishes: How Answering One Simple Question Can Make Your Dreams Come True, by Gay Hendricks

Forgive for Good: A Proven Prescription for Health and Happiness, by Fred Luskin

I'm Okay, You're a Brat: Setting the Priorities Straight and Freeing You from the Guilt and Mad Myths of Parenthood, by Susan Jeffers

Kitchen Table Wisdom: Stories that Heal, by Rachel Naomi Remen

The Last Lecture, by Randy Pausch

Loveability: Knowing How to Love and Be Loved, by Robert Holden

Loving What Is: Four Questions that Can Change Your Life, by Byron Katie

A New Earth: Awakening to Your Life's Purpose, by Eckhart Tolle

The Sacred Journey: You and Your Higher Self, by Lazaris

Self-Compassion, by Kristin Neff, Ph.D

Strong Fathers, Strong Daughters: 10 Secrets Every Father Should Know, by Meg Meeker

Way of the Peaceful Warrior: A Book that Changes Lives, by Dan Millman

The Way of the Superior Man: A Spiritual Guide to Mastering the Challenges of Women, Work, and Sexual Desire, by David Deida

Will You Still Love Me if I Don't Win?: A Guide for Parents of Young Athletes, by Christopher Andersonn with Barbara Andersonn

Wishes Fulfilled: Mastering the Art of Manifesting, by Wayne Dyer

You Can Heal Your Life, by Louise Hay

Workshops

Celebrating Men, Satisfying Women (for women only)—
www.understandmen.com

Financial Peace University—www.daveramsey.com/fpu

The Landmark Forum—www. landmarkworldwide.com

The New Warrior Training Adventure (for men only)—
www.mankindproject.org

Next Step to Being the Change—www.challengeday.org

The Shadow Process—www.thefordinstitute.com

Videos

I Am, by Tom Shadyac

Miss Representation, by Jennifer Siebel Newsom and Kimberlee
Acquaro

The Shadow Effect, featuring Debbie Ford, Deepak Chopra, Marianne Williamson, and others

The Shift, featuring Wayne Dyer

TED.com (any and all videos on this site, especially those by
Brené Brown, Elizabeth Gilbert, and Steve Jobs)

You Can Heal Your Life, featuring Louise Hay

Acknowledgments

I'm filled with a deep sense of gratitude as I reflect upon all of the amazing people in my life who have supported me with the creation of this book. First and foremost, Michelle Benoit Robbins, thank you for being the amazing woman, wife, and mother that you are. You're a miracle worker, and I'm so honored to get to spend my life in partnership with you. Thanks for holding down the fort in the midst of creation of this book and our move. I'm grateful for the incredible love, support, and magic you provide for me, the girls, and our life. I could not have written this book and could not do what I do without you. I am so lucky to be married to you. Samantha Benoit Robbins, thanks for your passion, your inspiration, and your love—you continue to teach me so much and I'm honored to be your daddy. Annarose Benoit Robbins, thanks for being the loving, cuddly, sweet soul that you are and for reminding me what truly matters in life. I love being your daddy and watching you grow.

Melanie Bates, what a blessing you have been in my life, for my business, and with this book. Your partnership, support, feedback, editing, and vision helped this come alive—it wouldn't have happened in the way and the time it did without you, your gifts, and your incredible support. Thank you! Michele Martin, thanks for believing in me, for your feedback, your wisdom, and your support. I feel honored and grateful to have you as my agent.

Richard Carlson, I miss you, brother, and wish you were still here with us in body. I appreciate all of the love, support, and mentorship you provided for me. And, I'm happy we're still connected through time and space. I feel your presence in my life and am grateful for it. Kris Carlson, thank you for your generosity. I appreciate your specific support and blessing with this book, with my work, and in my life. Thank you!

Reid Tracy, thank you for staying in touch with me over the years, for your patience, and for your continued interest in partnering with me. Louise Hay, thank you for your amazing work and for creating such a wonderful company with a beautiful mission. Patty Gift, thank you for your support and for choosing to work with me. Laura Gray, thank you for your partnership, your commitment, and your skill—you are a wonderful editor. Nancy Levin, Richelle Zizian, Christy Salinas, Jennifer Simmons, Elizabeth Kelley, Johanne Mahaffey, Margarete Nielsen, Kyle Thompson, Dani Riehl, Mollie Langer, Wioleta Gramek, Donna Abate, Stacey Smith, Erin Dupree, Heather Tate, Sally Mason, Shay Lawry, Shannon Godwin and the rest of the amazing team at Hay House—thank you for being such kind, warm, fun, and talented people to work with. I feel honored and grateful to be a part of the Hay House family.

Steve Sisgold, thank you for your guidance, and for those amazing sessions that created such healing, clarity, and peace for me. Amy Ahlers, thank you for your love, support, and enthusiasm. Christine Arylo, thank you for your creativity, passion, and vision. Lissa Rankin, thank you for your inspiration, the amazing introductions, and for all that you've taught me.

Lori Robbins, thank you for your courage, support, friendship, and love. You amaze me and I'm grateful to be your little brother. Rachel Cohen, thank you for your love, wisdom, and perspective. I love having you for a sister. Dad, thanks for all you taught me and gave me. Mom, thanks for the incredible lessons and your belief in me. Steve Farrell, thank you for always seeing me, "getting" me, and loving me through the years.

Theo Androus, thanks for being the kind of friend you are and the kind of man you are. I learn so much from you and continue to be grateful for our connection. Asa Siegel, thanks for being my brother for all of these years and for continuing to support me, believe in me, and be there for me. Chris Kyle, thank you for your brotherhood, support, and love. I'm grateful we are friends and appreciate having you in my life.

Gabrielle Bernstein, thank you for your light, passion, and inspiration. Lisa McLeod, thank you for your feedback and support. Rich Fettke, thank you for your continued guidance and friendship through the years and on this journey. Karen Drucker, thank you for your gifts, your inspiration, and your beautiful music. Juliet Funt, thank you for being my friend and success partner. Patty Koch, thank you for your love, support, and enthusiasm.

Fred Luskin, I'm grateful for your mentorship and generosity. Robert Holden, I'm so glad we've met and become friends—thank you for your amazing work and for your guidance. Dan Millman, your work and your books have inspired me for many years; I'm grateful to know you. Brené Brown, your work has touched me deeply and influenced this book and my work; thank you. Glennon Melton, thank you for your passion, love, and authenticity. Your writing and approach have had a big impact on me, my work, and on this book specifically.

Chris Andersonn, I continue to be deeply grateful for your presence and influence in my life over all of these years; thank you. Eleanor, I'm not sure I can even put into words the extent of my gratitude for you and the incredible work we have done together over the past few years. Cai Bristol, you are amazing and your work has had a profound impact on me personally and professionally.

To my many wonderful clients, thank you for allowing me to come into your organizations, speak at your events, and connect with your people. I feel honored, grateful, and humbled to be able to share my work, my insight, and my passion. Specifically to the clients who have brought me in multiple times in recent years, like Google, Wells Fargo, Gap, eBay, Schwab, Adobe, and others, thank you for trusting me, for allowing me to support your people, and for helping me support my family and do work that I love.

To all of those I didn't mention specifically—friends, family members, clients, colleagues, coaches, mentors, speakers, authors, teachers, teams, organizations, and others who've supported me with this book, along my path, and in my life and work—thank you for encouraging me, challenging me, teaching me, being there for me, and helping bring out the best in me.

And, finally, I want to thank and acknowledge myself for my willingness to show up, be real, put myself out there, push past my limits, and not let my gremlin stop me, and for being the passionate, loving, vulnerable man that I am. I'm grateful to be me, proud of myself and this book, and honored to be doing this work.

About the Author

Mike Robbins is the author of *Focus on the Good Stuff* and *Be Yourself, Everyone Else Is Already Taken,* which have been translated into 14 languages. He's a sought-after speaker who delivers keynotes and seminars around the world. Mike works with people, teams, and organizations, empowering them to appreciate themselves and each other, be real, work well together, produce results with ease, and keep things in perspective. His clients include some of the top organizations in the world, such as Google, Wells Fargo, Adobe, Gap, the U.S. Department of Labor, Charles Schwab, Twitter, the San Francisco Giants, eBay, and many more. Mike is a member of the National Speakers Association and one of less than 10 percent of the professional speakers worldwide to have earned the prestigious Certified Speaking Professional (CSP) designation.

Prior to his writing and speaking career, Mike was drafted by the New York Yankees out of high school, but chose instead to play baseball at Stanford University, where he pitched in the College World Series. After college, he played baseball professionally in the Kansas City Royals organization, until an injury ended his career while he was still in the minor leagues. He's been a regular contributor to *The Huffington Post* since 2008, and his work has been featured on *ABC News*, the Oprah radio network, *The Washington Post,* and many other media outlets.

Mike lives in the San Francisco Bay Area with his wife, Michelle, and their two daughters, Samantha and Rosie.

To learn more about Mike and his work, visit www .Mike-Robbins.com. You can also connect with him on Facebook (www.facebook.com/mikerobbinspage) and Twitter (@MikeDRobbins).

Hay House Titles of Related Interest

YOU CAN HEAL YOUR LIFE, the movie,
starring Louise Hay & Friends
(available as a 1-DVD program and an expanded 2-DVD set)
Watch the trailer at: www.LouiseHayMovie.com

THE SHIFT, the movie,
starring Dr. Wayne W. Dyer
(available as a 1-DVD program and an expanded 2-DVD set)
Watch the trailer at: www.DyerMovie.com

❀❀❀

THE ANSWER IS SIMPLE . . . LOVE YOURSELF, LIVE YOUR SPIRIT,
by Sonia Choquette

I CAN SEE CLEARLY NOW, by Dr. Wayne W. Dyer

LOVEABILITY: Knowing How to Love and Be Loved,
by Robert Holden, Ph.D.

*MIRACLES NOW: 108 Life-Changing Tools for Less Stress, More
Flow, and Finding Your True Purpose,* by Gabrielle Bernstein

All of the above are available at your local bookstore,
or may be ordered by contacting Hay House.

❀❀❀

We hope you enjoyed this Hay House book. If you'd like to receive our online catalog featuring additional information on Hay House books and products, or if you'd like to find out more about the Hay Foundation, please contact:

Hay House, Inc., P.O. Box 5100, Carlsbad, CA 92018-5100
(760) 431-7695 or (800) 654-5126
(760) 431-6948 (fax) or (800) 650-5115 (fax)
www.hayhouse.com® • www.hayfoundation.org

❀ ❀ ❀

Published and distributed in Australia by:
Hay House Australia Pty. Ltd., 18/36 Ralph St., Alexandria NSW 2015
Phone: 612-9669-4299 • *Fax:* 612-9669-4144 • www.hayhouse.com.au

Published and distributed in the United Kingdom by:
Hay House UK, Ltd., Astley House, 33 Notting Hill Gate, London W11 3JQ
Phone: 44-20-3675-2450 • *Fax:* 44-20-3675-2451• www.hayhouse.co.uk

Published and distributed in the Republic of South Africa by:
Hay House SA (Pty), Ltd., P.O. Box 990, Witkoppen 2068
Phone/Fax: 27-11-467-8904 • www.hayhouse.co.za

Published in India by: Hay House Publishers India,
Muskaan Complex, Plot No. 3, B-2, Vasant Kunj, New Delhi 110 070
Phone: 91-11-4176-1620 • *Fax:* 91-11-4176-1630 • www.hayhouse.co.in

Distributed in Canada by: Raincoast Books,
2440 Viking Way, Richmond, B.C. V6V 1N2
Phone: 1-800-663-5714 • *Fax:* 1-800-565-3770 • www.raincoast.com

❀ ❀ ❀

Take Your Soul on a Vacation

Visit www.HealYourLife.com® to regroup, recharge,
and reconnect with your own magnificence.
Featuring blogs, mind-body-spirit news,
and life-changing wisdom from Louise Hay and friends.

Visit www.HealYourLife.com today!